The History of the
West Cumberland Potteries
Volume II

Florence Sibson

British Library Cataloguing in Publication data
A British Library CIP record is available.

A copy of this book has been placed with the British Library

ISBN 978 0 9560986 0 3

Published by
Cope Publishing
9 Commonside
Distington
CA14 4PU

Printed and designed by Titus Wilson and Son, Kendal, Cumbria.
Photographs by the author Florence Sibson

I dedicate this book to my lovely granddaughter Laura Sibson

This is a limited edition of 750 copies.

This is copy No. 100

Florence V. Dickson

CONTENTS

Chapter III

Nineteenth century

Appendices

ILLUSTRATIONS AND DOCUMENTS

Teawares

Names and Initials on the eggs.

ACKNOWLEDGEMENTS

First and foremost my proof reader and friend retired Local Studies Librarian, at the Whitehaven Record Office, Miss Anne Dick, Whitehaven.

Secondly my neighbour Donald G. Scarrott who untangled my I.T. problems.

Thirdly the late Derek Chitty of Hest Bank who encouraged me to get started with I.T. and Digital Photography.

The Lowther family trustees of Penrith, especially Lady Caroline Lowther, President of the Friends of Whitehaven Museum, for her support and encouragement during the publication of both of my books. The members of Whitehaven Soroptimists for their unwavering support at all times.

My two sisters Iris and Hazel for their help and encouragement.

My many friends, also potaholics, who have allowed me to photograph their pots and have given me permission to publish them in this book.

Dr. Geoffrey Godden, Mr Henry Sandon, Mr Terry Lockett, Mr Eric Knowles, Miss Gaye Blake-Roberts, Mr and Mrs Peter Mobbs, Mr and Mrs Bob Slatcher, Mrs Joyce Chitty, Mrs Barbara Sandon, Mr and Mrs James Knowles, Mrs Kay Dickson, Mrs Sheila Bidgood, Mrs Barbara Blenkinship, Mrs Beatrice Stocks, Dr Sonia and Mr Brian Parkinson, Mr Robin Emerson.

Mr Christopher Cross, (property owner), The Staff of Carlisle and Whitehaven County Record Offices, The Headmaster, staff and pupils of St. Bees School, Mr and Mrs Tom Mossop and family, Miss Susan Palmer, Manager and her staff of The Beacon, Whitehaven, Mr and Mrs Geoffrey Wilkinson, Sally Connor, Jim and Robert Bennett, Distington, Mr and Mrs Robert Pearson, St. Bees, the Curator and staff of the Helena Thompson Museum, Workington, the Lister family of Fox House Farm, Mr and Mrs Jim Wilson, Crossbarrow Farm, Clifton, Workington.

My tutors in I.T. Maggie Clime, I.T. Ignorant, Keswick School. Margaret Storey, Cockermouth School Clait, and especially Janet McHugh and Clive Wilson, of 'Over 55s' at Beckstone Primary School, Harrington, also the Headmaster Mr David Warbrick.

My I.T. papers and inks were purchased from Messrs Mill Tech., Whitehaven. My digital photographs were developed by Messrs Boots. I used Microsoft Word 2003 and XP on my computer, the photographs were scanned using my Epsom Perfection 3170 photo, whilst my printer is an Epsom Stylus Photo R.300.

Shaun, Bryan and Steve at Messrs Titus Wilson & Son my printers.

Last but not least, the main potoholic in my life, Donald my husband. He has a nose for finding my pots!!! I'm grateful for his support and encourgement at all times.

INTRODUCTION

'I am pleased with the manufacture you have of earthenware-where ships are, the whole world is the market and things once began cannot in that case be hindered from advancing'.

Sir John Lowther of Whitehaven wrote these words to his steward William Gilpin on the 8th March, 1697.

One hundred years later Sir John's prophesy became a reality; Whitehaven's sailing ships were taking our pots as far afield as Canada, the Caribbean and the Americas.

The ceramic historians neglected Cumberland mainly owing to its geographical isolation which lasted even into the nineteenth century. King Charles II had granted mineral rights to the Lowther family of Penrith and this sparsely populated region was transformed into a thriving community when eventually the valuable coal seams began to be extensively mined.

Fortunately the Earl of Lonsdale deposited the Lowther family documents relating to West Cumberland in the Castle at Carlisle, during the war years (1939-45) for safe keeping, then later he decided that the documents should remain there so that they be readily accessible to local historians.

More than two decades have past since I first investigated and recorded the pots of my beloved county. Volume I, published in 1991 showed the whereabouts of the potteries and the names of the families associated with them. However since then a great deal has been discovered, uncovered and recorded.

In the mid 1990s the then Curator at The Beacon, Whitehaven, Gillian Finley asked permission on behalf of The Friends of Whitehaven Museum to reprint Volume I.

I was busy sorting through files at the time, in order to talk to a group of ceramicists at a seminar in Carlisle, organised by Mrs Wendy Mitton. I therefore invited Gillian and the Chairman of the Friends of Whitehaven Museum, Mr Ian Rule to visit my home for a preview.

It was only then I realised I had to publish another book, the material contained in Volume I, needed to be updated. Research will always be like this. New material is periodically uncovered. The electronics available today should make it easier, digital photography, computers etc. It has been a labour of love, washing and recording my shards together with my many battles with my computer!

In Volume I the discovery of the three slipware dishes made exciting reading however the new knowledge that the 'Clifton Dish' was made by local potter James Tunstall is rewarding.

The creamware and saltglazing kiln which came to light in 1994 in 'Douglas Burn', (behind Whitehaven Market Place), is equally rewarding. When Christopher Cross the owner of the property brought me the two creamware mugs, beautifully engine turned, which had been unearthed by two mechanical diggers nearly unscathed, I was astounded. Then we found more…..!

Also the important documents provided by two colleagues in America Professor George L. Miller and Asst. Prof. Dr. Anne Smart-Martin who were looking for a contact in West Cumberland 'concerning a retailer' made me realise how fortunate I have been. A letter dated 1772 described the Whitehaven creamware which was shipped out on *The Milham*, whilst their invoices for 1836 give the prices and descriptions of the Whitehaven pots being produced at this period.

Likewise the rare copies of the local newspapers printed in 1819 and 1820 provided by Mr and Mrs Robert Pearson of St. Bees which give the cargoes and destinations, world wide, for our Whitehaven Pottery.

I realise *my maker* put me on this earth to do this work. I hope you enjoy reading about my finds.

CHAPTER I

THE SEVENTEENTH CENTURY

The first potter recorded in West Cumberland was Thomas Foorth of Dearham when on the 23rd April, 1637 he registered the birth of his son Henry and described himself as a potter on the Bridekirk church parish registers, page 39. C.R.O. Carlisle.

Potters in Whitehaven old town

February, 1674 Sir John Lowther the local land owner instructed his steward Thomas Tickell to engage Edward Gibson, (a brick maker), to work in Whitehaven. It was obvious Sir John Lowther was ambitious for Edward Gibson to succeed as he even obtained a crate of *Dutch tiles* for him to copy.

By November 1686 Edward Gibson was producing 40,000 bricks a year and according to Professor D.R. Ainsworth (The Records of Social and Economic History, New Series VII) Edward Gibson was also producing roof tiles, (the long square type), also pots which he interbaked with the tiles.

In July 1689 Jeremy Lyons a potter from Rainhill, Liverpool was invited to Whitehaven. He was encouraged to experiment with the Whitehaven clay; he used the local coal to fire his pots. (A plentiful commodity, as Sir John Lowther owned the many local small coal mines). However, he soon discovered the coal was too keen on *caking* which spoiled his pots, so a disillusioned Jeremy Lyons left the area.

Sir John Lowther, now living in London, and hearing of the success of the various other potters was ambitious for a production of red ware, tiles, stoneware and white ware and after receiving encouraging news from his new steward John Spedding regarding the suitability of our clays he contracted with a Staffordshire workman at Burslem at 2s per week, the date February, 1698. The Staffordshire man was Aaron Wedgwood, great uncle to the now famous master potter Josiah Wedgwood. Aaron was born in 1671, son of Thomas of Burslem b.1644.

Trials were held at Aikbank, a hill above the town and within its boundaries, using the copper furnaces. Yet again the trials were unsuccessful. Aaron blamed the failure to a lack of skilled workmen. I'm certain he would mean that none of the local work men would be skilled *kiln firers*.

Aaron did not leave West Cumberland. Shortly after he married Margaret Tunstall, a lady's maid. They went to live at Rebton (now known as Ribton), near Cockermouth where he joined the potters of Dearham. (See later chapters). In December, 1697 William Gilpin Sir John Lowther's Steward had written to his master in London with reference to tests for the manufacture of clay tobacco pipes in the town of Whitehaven.

The correspondence records that '*suitable fine clay had been found which though dried white was apt to burn red through being tainted with vitriol and okra with which it abounds*'. However, later, clay was discovered which gave them '*hope of a better success*'. (C.R.O. Carlisle, the Lowther Family Trust).

By the 1st March, 1698, Sir John Lowther had two tobacco houses built in Hodgson's Croft, (today's Market Place, in Whitehaven).

Thomas Birch tenanted the first pipe house No. 16 (1701-1706) and Abel Robinson No. 17 (1698-1700). The latter was taken over in 1701 by Frenchman Jon Boulain.

Boulain must have been successful as in 1704 he moved into a new house with stable in nearby Preston Street, yearly rental two guineas.

According to these same Lowther documents Thomas Birch was still making pipes in 1723. However the 1762 Whitehaven census shows his son Caleb has succeeded his father. (Daniel Hay Collection, C.R.O. Whitehaven).

Caleb Birch was a pew owner at the Presbyterian Church in the Market Place, Whitehaven. Courtesy of Anne Dick, '*Whitehaven United Reformed Church, 1695-1995, with a supplement published in 2005*'.

 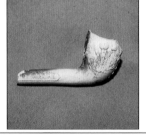 

The word 'don't'	The word 'cadge'	'WHITEHAVEN' along the stem
Cumbria dialect for 'Don't borrow'		

These incomplete pipes depicting the Prince of Wales Feathers on the pipe bowl were excavated. The whole pipe illustrated above was discovered along the local shoreline. I was given permission to photograph it in 1985 by the owner, a member of Moresby Church Mother's Union; it had belonged to her husband.

Illustrated below is a copy of a document showing the letting of the clay pipe houses in Hodgson's Croft by the Lowther family in 1704 C.R.O. Carlisle.

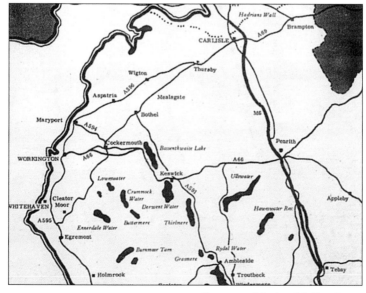

Courtesy of the Lowther family trustees.

The following map shows the area covered by the History of the West Cumberland Potteries-Volume II.

Courtesy of the late Mr Ron Jones.

CHAPTER II

THE EIGHTEENTH CENTURY

Undoubtedly the most important items of Cumberland post medieval pottery which I have discovered up to now are the 3 large slip decorated dishes which are described in detail in the following paragraphs.

Firstly the Stephen Shaw dish now housed in The British Museum, London which is initialled S.S. with slip, onto the clay body, to either side of the Royal Arms which are impressed on the front in the centre (an illegal act at this time however Stephen Shaw was in far flung Cumberland). Impressed into the clay on the reverse are the words By Stephen Shaw 1725.

Hugh Tait, at one time Keeper of Ceramics at the British Museum and Harry Fancy previously Curator of the Whitehaven Museum, record that the 'Stephen Shaw' dish was given to the owner of the Distington Museum (a Mr J.R. Wallace) by a Mr. John Ritson. I have been trying to find out for some time who John Ritson was and how he obtained this 'Stephen Shaw' dish. From church records at the Whitehaven Record Office I discovered John Ritson was the father-in-law of John R. Wallace, the owner of the Distington Private Museum. John Ritson died in 1837 aged 95 years old.

John Ritson's daughter Elizabeth christened her son Joseph. Later, as a grown man, he added the name Ritson, he being the Distington museum owner, now to be known as Mr Joseph Ritson Wallace. He in turn christened his son Joseph Ritson Paitson Wallace. Paitson being a name associated with the West Cumberland Potteries. (See nineteenth century, chapter III, page 52, with reference to the new owners of the Whitehaven Pottery).

I recorded John Ritson's will. He left his belongings, credits etc., to his daughter and grandson (J.R. Wallace), so possibly this is how the 'Stephen Shaw' dish came to his private museum at Distington, West Cumbria.

In his Directory of Cumberland of 1797 William Hutchinson makes reference to the fact that a Reverend Joseph Ritson was Incumbent at Dearham in 1736. This is also engraved on a window in Dearham Church.

At the time of John Ritson's christening in 1742 at All Saints Church, Cockermouth, his father being Henry, the Reverend Joseph Ritson was baptising 2 daughters at the same church. The Reverend Joseph Ritson gave his occupation as Vicar of Egremont and Schoolmaster of Cockermouth. We must presume John Ritson had grown up knowing of the close association between these two men.

I wonder did the Reverend Joseph Ritson receive this 'Stephen Shaw' inscribed dish at Dearham or Egremont, then later give it to John Ritson for his son-in-law's museum at Distington, West Cumberland? Bernard Rackham records that the 'Stephen Shaw' dish was exhibited at the Burlington Fine Arts Club in 1914 (Cat. C17).

Further research has revealed a second large slipware dish from the same mould. It is in the *Dr. Glaisher Collection of Pottery and Porcelain,* in the Fitzwilliam Museum, Cambridge. Scant details have been recorded about this dish except by Berhard Rackham in his *Catalogue of 'The Glaisher Collection of Pottery and Porcelain' Volume I, Item No. 199, page 34.*

Rackham describes this second dish as follows.

Light, slip only, used for decoration. The inside wholly filled with an incorrect version of the Royal Arms, with crown, lion and unicorn supporters, and lion below. The shield shows in the first quarter a lion rampart above three lions passant, in the second chequers, the third a heart, and the fourth three fleur de lys. On the underside, numerous impressions from a cut stick. Diam. 15½ ins., 39.3cm. First half of the 18th century. Lot 190B, S. March, 16th, 1928.

According to Rackham the moulds for dishes of this type are formed by pressing the clay over a convex earthenware mould on which the design has been incised.

Personally I am confident that a third large slipware marriage dish which I discovered in a farmhouse at Crossbarrow, near Clifton, West Cumbria, and recorded, is from the same mould. This Clifton Marriage Dish is initialled I T with slip, (within the Royal Arms in the centre panel), possibly JAMES TUNSTALL of Dearham. I am certain it had been made for the marriage of Edward Harrington to Mary Thompson on the 18th July, 1767 at Bridekirk Church. They both lived at Great Broughton.

According to Dr. Geoffrey Godden there was no 'J' in the Roman alphabet up until 1820, therefore before 1820, potters and clockmakers signed their work 'I' be they James, John or Joseph. The Royal Arms on this dish date from the reign of George III, (1760-1800).

The front cover of the Sale Catalogue of the contents of the Cumberland Private Museum at Distington, Workington, Cumberland.

No. 4244
Old English Pottery Dish signed and dated "By Stephen Shaw 1725"

The Clifton Marriage Dish showing the initials E.H.M.and in the centre I.T. i.e. James Tunstall the local potter. Made for Edward Harrington and Mary Thompson, who married at Bridekirk Church on the 18th July, 1767.

The Reverse, incised into the clay 'Clifton Dish'.

On the 7th February, 1757 the Reverend Joseph Ritson signed the will of Moses Tunstall who was the father of James, also a potter.

Ceramic historians have recorded a failed litigation case, involving the Staffordshire potters Ralph and Stephen Shaw. Evidence exists proving that Ralph went to live and work in France. However the whereabouts of Stephen has remained a mystery up until now. The existence of the first large dish, housed at one time in a local Cumberland museum, together with my lucky find of a third dish, (from an identical mould), seems to me to prove that Stephen not only fled Staffordshire and came to West Cumberland, but worked at Dearham for a short time, leaving his mould with Moses Tunstall, (father

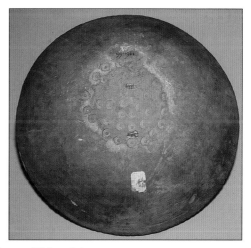

The Fitzwilliam Museum Slipware Dish and the reverse.

of James). It was James who used the mould many years later (perhaps only on one occasion) to make the Clifton Marriage Dish and put his initials within the Royal Arms on the front.

In March, 1991 I received a letter from the Assistant Keeper of Applied Art at The Fitzwilliam Museum re their dish which had been purchased by Dr. J.W.L. Glaisher at Sotheby's on the l6th March, 1928 (lot 190B) and was attributed to Staffordshire along with other hump-moulded slipware dishes in Bernard Rackham's *Catalogue of the Glaisher Collection*, 1935, She went on to say 'Until your lucky discovery of the inscribed Clifton Dish there was no reason to associate it with Cumbria'. The label has now been changed to provide the correct attribution, as we know it, up-to-press.

The Stephen Shaw Dish in the British Museum.

The reverse incised into the clay By Stephen Shaw 1725.

THE TUNSTALL, WEDGWOOD AND LISTER FAMILIES OF WEST CUMBERLAND

Moses Tunstall was born in Burslem, Staffordshire on the l8th July, 1700, son of John. He was the first member of the family of potters to settle in West Cumberland. He married Sarah Jackson of Driffield, Derbyshire in 1730. He described himself on the church registers as a potter. He died at Greysouthen, in West Cumberland and was buried at St. Bridget's Church, Brigham on the 7th February, 1757. His wife was also buried there on the 30th March, 1778, possibly the same person as Sarah Tunstall, *Widow of Crossbarrow* recorded in the registers of the neighbouring parish of Workington. Crossbarrow was where I discovered the Clifton Marriage Dish in 1989.

Their son James was born in l8th August, 1741 and christened at St. Mungo's Church in Dearham. (Dearham, where Aaron Wedgwood, the first of Cumberland, lived and worked at this time and where the Reverend Joseph Ritson was Vicar).

According to the St. Bees Church registers for 5th January, 1766 No. 289, a Matthew

Sibson and James Tunstall (potter), are witnesses at a wedding at the church. This is surely the same James Tunstall who made the Clifton marriage dish. Was he working alongside Aaron Wedgwood and Stephen Shaw, for the merchant Peter How at St. Bees? This would allow him another opportunity to gain possession of the Stephen Shaw mould!

Another son Aaron, was born to Moses and Sarah, on the 24th July, 1747. (Presumably called after Aaron Wedgwood, their neighbour and fellow potter). James married Ann Pattinson/Patrickson at St. James Church, Whitehaven on the 4th January, 1767. At the time of his death on the 17th October, 1780 it is recorded that Aaron Tunstall is living at Crossbarrow. Presumably his widowed mother had been living with her son, up until the time of her death, two years earlier.*

John Tunstall, (son of James and Ann who now lived at Fox House, Great Broughton), describes himself as a farmer and potter when christening his daughter. John Tunstall was born 15th September, 1782 and was christened at Bridekirk Church however he was buried at St. Bridget's, Brigham, 8th May, 1860. His gravestone in Brigham Churchyard records the death of 5 of his children in 1827. John Tunstall came to Whitehaven in 1813 as partner to Mr Joseph Goulding of the Glass House Pottery enterprize. (see Agate Tobacco Jar initialled and dated J.T. 1853, described in the section headed Miscellaneous.)

According to Professor D.R.Hainsworth's transcriptions of Sir John Lowther's family records re Whitehaven, Aaron Wedgwood of Staffordshire was engaged in 1698, to make trials to try to make fine red/creamware pottery at Aikbank, an area within the town's boundaries. This same correspondence, between Sir John Lowther and his agent John Spedding, claimed that *a lack of skilled workmen deemed the project to failure.*

Lease of Dearham Mill   *Courtesy of the Lowther Family Trust, CRO Carlisle.*

---

* *family documents loaned to me by Sally Connor, Whitehaven. Church records from County Record Office, Whitehaven.*

However Aaron did not leave West Cumberland but married a lady's maid Margaret Tunstall and they settled down firstly at Rebton (now Ribton), Camerton, near the town of Cockermouth, then finally in a cottage at Harker Marsh, Broughton Moor. Their sons Thomas, William, Moses and Aaron followed in their father's footsteps, eventually renting a much larger building, Dearham Mill and gained permission to extract clay on nearby commons. They were producing the earthenware requirements for the rural community i.e. farm troughs, field drains and making domestic pottery.

Dearham Mill today.

Coat of Arms of the Cumberland Wedgwoods. (Courtesy of the Headmaster, Netherhall School, Maryport).

In 1754 Sir John Lowther sent, once more, for a third member of the Wedgwood family. This time it was Aaron the III of Cumberland who came to make trials at Scilly Banks, an area close to Whitehaven where fine clay had been discovered.

Seated in the centre Mr Phillip Wedgwood. Governors of Flimby School in 1903. (Courtesy of Jean Sanders, Whitehaven).

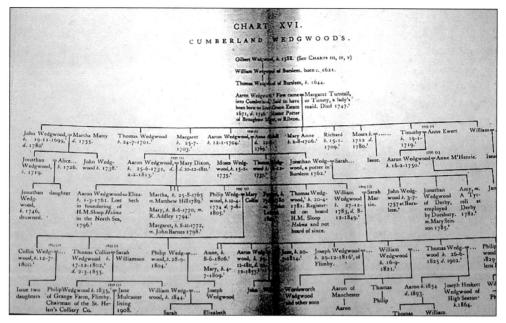

THE CUMBERLAND WEDGWOODS' FAMILY TREE.
(Courtesy of Miss Gaye Blake-Roberts, Curator, The Wedgwood Museum, Barleston).

(C.R.O. Carlisle, Courtesy of the Lowther Family Trust).

This document shows Aaron Wedgwood III securing the lease to extract clay for 21 years at Scilly Banks, Whitehaven in 1754. In 1757 Aaron Wedgwood III married a local girl Mary Dixon, at St. James Church, in Whitehaven. They later christened a child at Holy Trinity Church, Whitehaven.

In 2004 the members of The Northern Ceramic Society were recommended to read a book published in 2002 by the Science Museum, London, entitled *R.R. Angerstein, a Swedish Industrial Spy who travelled throughout Great Britain in 1753-56.*

Angerstein records *seeing men coming out of the very hot kilns, who wound hoops of hazel birch around their bodies.* With further research, I discovered that the sap of hazel birch contains the oil of wintergreen. These kilnmen, working in intense heat, were therefore protecting their bodies from the cooler outside air until their body temperature cooled down, hopefully staving off any future aches and pains! Oil of wintergreen, when mixed with sugar, makes Cough Candy another old homeopathic remedy for a cold and a saleable product.

At this period Whitehaven was part of the trade triangle, our ships called at Arnside, in the south of the county, where they collected gunpowder for the African mines. They then collected slave persons for the sugar and tobacco plantations in the Caribbean and Virginia, U.S.A. They returned carrying tobacco leaf, liquid sugar and rum.

In 1712 Sir James Lowther built a sugar refining house on Whitehaven harbour. It was run by a Mr. Barwise, a distiller of Workington. The sugar was purified using ox-blood and lime. In Whitehaven, we have

Amherst Japan pattern, mark I.W.

The Marseillaise pattern this is the common pattern.

The rare version shows a lady with 2 children.

two quays on our harbour called the Lime Tongue and the Sugar Tongue. Treacle is a by-product, and our Whitehaven Treacle Jars are family heirlooms, as are our Rum Butter Bowls which come out at family christenings in West Cumbria.

This illustration from Rochefort's *Histoire naturelle et morale des Antibes, Paris, 1681,* is a drawing of a scene from sugar production in the French Antilles, but could be from any other Caribbean Island.

The horsemill is drawn by an oxen. The shaft goes into a pivot hole of a horizontal guide beam supported by braced posts, beyond, the circular walk of the dray animals. The artist has omitted the posts. The posts limit the size of the walk and consequently the leverage that could be employed in turning the roller. The unsupported length of the guide beam is limited so its value as a brace, in the improved Horsemill system was abolished. The early windmills were invented by English millwrights early in the 18th century however most European countries acquired a foothold in the Caribbean by the 19th century.

The earliest sugar presses show mangles were used to extract the sap from the stripped sugar cane stalks. However later machinery was developed that continued to be the basic element of all cane crushing throughout the 19th century.

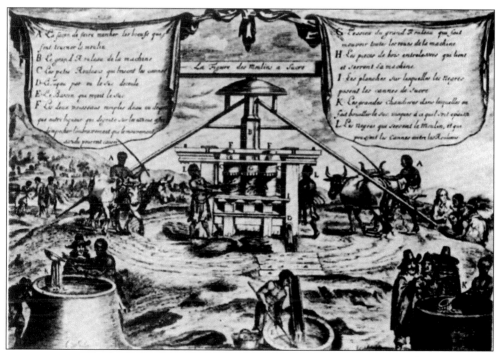

A Sugar Mill in operation in the Caribbean.

Angerstein visited St. Bees and recorded the existence and whereabouts, of an Iron Foundry, for the first time, at Low Mill, near Thornhill.

On page 288 After scouring the iron scrap is placed in specially thrown pots 12" high, 8" in diameter. Later he states *a man is paid 2s. per week to keep the fires burning and for throwing the pots which cannot be used more than once.*

On page 306 *The requirements for pots would be approximately 40 pots per week. A man could not live on 2s per week so this job would be part time.*

When Sir James rescinded Aaron Wedgwood's lease on the property at Scilly Banks, Whitehaven, in 1754, Aaron must have gone to work for Peter How at Low Mill, near Thornhill. This is the address he gave in the St. Bees church registers when christening two of his children in 1763 and 1765. However he still retained the lease giving him the right to dig for clay on 4 nearby commons for 21 years (the norm for all mineral rights on any Lowther Estate.)

Peter How was a wealthy Whitehaven merchant and entrepreneur. Part owner of at least 20 ships. He had a tallow factory and snuff mill in Whitehaven, and was agent for the French for the purchase of fine tobacco leaf in the Caribbean. He was also Collector of Taxes for the King, so had a ready supply of cash which pleased the Ships' Captains, whereas the Lowthers had to wait until their goods were sold before getting their London Bills.

The IGI (Whitehaven Record Office) shows Peter How married Annie Walker of Moresby on 15/03/1729. They had a daughter Margaret who married Mr Anthony Benn and a son Peter Junior who became the Vicar of the local Harrington Church.

For his second wife Peter How then married Christian Spedding, widow, (she was the second wife of Lowther Spedding), Peter had now married into the local gentry. (The Lowther and Spedding families). They married at Holy Trinity Church in Whitehaven, 28/08/1755.

The following facts were obtained from documents in The Beacon Museum in Whitehaven.

Peter How was described in the London Papers of this period as *Receiver General of the Land Tax, Window Tax and Excise for the County of Cumberland and Westmorland* upwards of 20 years and for 40 years one of the principal Merchants in the North of England. He was Agent to the French in Virginia from 1738.

These were wonder years for the port of Whitehaven, (which comprised the coastline from Millom to Maryport at this period of time). Imports in 1742 were 81% above the 1738-40 level and 144% above 1743-44. Whitehaven passed Bristol, Liverpool and the combined Clyde ports, to be for a few years the leading Tobacco Port after London. Peter How bought the superior grades from the James and York River plantations which merited premium prices. The leaf from the Potomac and Eastern shores of Maryland he sold to the French.

On the 26th March, 1753 The Rt. Hon. Earl of Egremont, owner of the Leconfield Estates, in West Cumberland, leased Bransty Rocks, Scarrs and Salt Pans, (steads), for 26 years to Peter How and others, as well as the Iron Mines in Egremont for 26 years 5 months and 2 days, at a rent of £50 or 18d. per ton.

In 1763, with the return of peace after the seven years war, Peter How seems to have reverted to his primary connection with George Fitzgerald the Irishman. Thus when Fitzgerald went bankrupt in December, 1759 Peter How was exposed. He survived the immediate blow. He struggled on until the end of 1763, before becoming bankrupt himself for £40,000. His collapse was a blow to the whole town of Whitehaven, but especially to Aaron Wedgwood who had been employed by Peter How, since 1754 when Wedgwood signed the lease issued by Sir John Lowther giving him permission to extract clay for 21 years from 4 commons around Whitehaven namely, Moresby, Hensingham, Preston Quarter and Distington.

Peter How died in 1772. Litigation followed, which was on going until 1792. Records prove Aaron Wedgwood left Low Mill and went to live in the Allerdale area of West Cumberland, where he christened a son Phillip, in 1774, according to the Workington (Allerdale) registers.

Peter How was buried in St. Nicholas churchyard, Whitehaven, on the 30th September, 1772.

In the 1762 Census of Whitehaven (*C.R.O. Whitehaven*), John Douglas is listed as potter, living and working in the Market Place, in the area where excavations took place in 1994 which uncovered a kiln, also saltglazed and creamware pots and shards.

Sir James Lowther was annoyed when he discovered rich Whitehaven merchant John Gale was letting off, to small businesses, parts of the Old Hall, Market Place, Whitehaven, which he had let to Gale in 1664 for 100yrs at a nominal rent. In the county records John Douglas is mentioned as one of Gale's tenants.

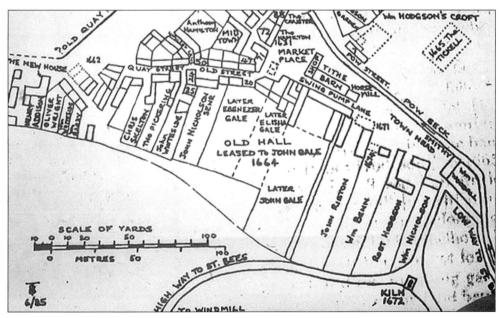

Andrew Pelin's Map of Whitehaven, 1698 Courtesy of Blake Tyson, Oxford Polytechnic
A.M.S. Transactions The Early Development of Whitehaven Before 1700.

Next we introduce the Lister family of potters, Fox House Farm (the Pot Kiln) Broughton Moor.

Jona Lister christened his daughter on the 7th January, 1802 and he described himself as a potter and recorded the above address on the church records. (C.R.O. Carlisle).

Meantime, in the same church, in baptism records for his daughter, John Tunstall, records that he was also living and working at Fox House (the Pot Kiln) and described himself as farmer and potter. However he left Fox House Farm in 1813 to start the Glass House Pottery in Preston Street, The Ginns, Whitehaven.

Tobacco Jar or Biscuit Barrel signed underneath J. Docherty.

This item can be seen in the Helena Thompson Museum, Workington.

The potteries of Harker Marsh (the Wedgwood home) and Fox House farm (the Pot Kiln), are separated by only one field. Whilst Dearham Mill (the other pottery in this area which was rented by Aaron Wedgwood's four sons), is barely 2 miles away. The pots which have survived are of excellent quality and glaze.

The pots are well made and show a superb manganese glaze over a yellow clay body.

When I'm asked to visualise the ceramics made in the eighteenth century my mind immediately conjures up images of country objects (some slip decorated), Delft (tin glazed), and creamware, delicately engine-turned and sprigged, also the scraffiti patterns or inscriptions, on saltglazed items. These are usually very rare objects, so you can imagine my surprise when a local lady, Jean Sanders, brought her 18th century creamware teapot to show me which was inscribed to a local girl Ester Saul, Beckfoot.

Astonishingly the timing of her visit, coincided with a visit from Sheila Bidgood, (expert on inscriptions on pots), also a telephone call late one evening, from the antiques expert Eric Knowles with reference to a creamware teapot inscribed *Whitehaven*, which had been stolen. Sheila Bidgood had been to Gloucestershire to see this teapot. She said it was housed in a disused Aeroplane Hanger, the only item of creamware amongst 4,000 stolen articles of pottery and porcelain. Sheila had brought her card index, of inscriptions on pots, and these proved three more creamware teapots with local inscriptions, existed. This made a total of five, as follows:-

1. Ester Saul, Beckfoot
2. Mary Saul, Beckfoot (sold by Messrs Phillips, L'dn., 1986, lot 147).
3. Susanna Drewry, Weary Hall, 1769
4. Molly Drewry, Weary Hall, (sold by Messrs Christies, London, 11th Oct., 1971, lot 47).
5. Samuel Abbot and Margrett Bowman, Whitehaven, 1770.

Recorded Antecedent	Children	Grandchildren	Great Grandchildren	Greatx2 Grandchildren	Greatx3 Grandchildren
JOHN HARRIS of Greysouthen (Mentioned in 1670)	1 THOMAS ?-1736 of Eaglesfield m 1670 RUTH STUBBS 1665-1745/6	1 JOHN 1691-1709			
		2 MARY 1693-? m JOSEPH ROBINSON ?-1742			
		3 RICHARD 1697-1716			
		4 JOSEPH 1700/1-1736 of Lamplugh m MARY POMSOMBY 1726-1757	1 JONATHAN I 1729-? of The Green Lamplugh m 1771 ESTHER SAUL of Holme	1 MARY 1771-? m DAN DUNGLINSON	1 JONATHAN III Jnr 1808-1855 m 1837 SARAH HALL MASON ?-1891
			2 SARAH	2 ANN 1774-? m CLERK of Bankhead nr Maryport	2 ESTHER 15/4-1892 (Unmarried)
				3 JANE 1776-?	3 JOSEPH ?-1882 m 1839 ELIZA HALL of Manchester
				4 SARAH 1779-? m CHRIS ROBINSON of Eaglesfield	4 MARY ?-1902 (Unmarried)
				5 JOSEPH 1781-? m DINAH BOADLE	5 SARAH ANN ?-1853 m CHARLES WHITE of Glasgow
				6 JONATHAN II 1783-1869	ELIZA 1831-?
			3 JOSEPH 1732-? of Eaglesfield & Lamplugh m MARY WILKINSON of Brandlinghill	1 JOHN 1760-1790 m ANN DICKENSON	1 RACHEL (No records)
			MARY POWE	2 JOSEPH 1763- (a Sea Captain died at Monsarrat)	2 MARY 1818-1894 "Kept house for her brother after his wife's death. This is 'Granty' who brought up the 5 Girls at Derwent Bank."
				3 JONATHAN died at sea	3 JOSEPH WILLIAM 1820-1892 m 1846 ANN BIGLAND 1820-1857
		5 HANNAH ?-? m JOSEPH JOHNSON of Pardshaw		4 ISAAC 1768-? m HANNA FAWCETT of Cockermouth	
		6 JANE 1704-(Pre 1776) m ANTHONY SAUL of Lamplugh 2 m SUSANNAH PEARSON 1776		5 PONSONBY 1771-? m 1802 SARAH DIXON of Toddle	
	2 WILLIAM	7 WILLIAM 1706-1785 of Lamplugh & Maryport m 1734 HANNAH WATSON ?-1785 of Broughton		6 MARY 1775-? m JOHN ROBINSON of Eaglesfield	
	3 JOSEPH ?-1716 of Pardshaw m 1709 MARY ROBINSON 1687-1767 of Pardshaw	1 SARAH 1711-?		7 WILLIAM 1782-1829 of Lamplugh m 1815 SARAH OSTLE of Broughton	

*Portrait at the Old Bakehouse

Family tree of Ester Saul and John Harris. His family owned the Harris Thread Mills, Cockermouth. A very wealthy Cumberland Quaker family.

I now give details of the Ester Saul teapot and its close association with West Cumberland. I wish to quote from the diary of a local man Isaac Fletcher of Underwood, Loweswater 1756-1781 (a Quaker), edited by Angus J.L. Winchester published by the C. and W.A. and A. Soc. Page 232:

Thurs., 7th March, 1771 'went with wife to Jonathan Harris (his wife's brother) and Ester Saul's wedding. Came home in the evening, very cold, sharp frost.'

(Beckfoot, Allonby, West Cumberland, is well known as being the site of a Quaker Meeting House and burial ground). I was indeed fortunate to handle, photograph and truthfully record the details of this first teapot inscribed Ester Saul.

The illustrations show the inscription and highlight the poor quality of the finished article which leaves a lot to be desired.

Inscription and part print.

The lid.

The pot does not appear to be the work of one of the expert craftsmen employed by the master potter Josiah Wedgwood. I feel certain this one and the fifth teapot came from moulds secreted out of Josiah's Staffordshire factory.

A transfer print on the front of this teapot shows a sailor handing over money to a lady. Recorded by ceramic historians as '*The Sailor's Return*'. According to experts, this is the rare version. It depicts his loving wife, in her best dress, greeting

The initials M.D are shown between the grass and the foliage (to the right of the hem of the ladies dress) which is to the left of the base of the teapot handle terminal.

him on the harbour side. Perhaps his ship had captured '*The Acapulco*' the Spanish Treasure ship, laden with Spanish Dollars from their silver mines in South America, so the purse he is offering her is his share of the bounty!

As these are the initials of Mary Dixon, later to become the wife of Aaron Wedgwood (III), can we presume Mary Dixon put her initials on this teapot? According to the experts the great Josiah Wedgwood allowed no engravers to print their names on any of his pots.

I feel certain Aaron Wedgwood III of Cumberland had somehow managed to obtain some of Josiah's moulds. I have made note of a similar occurrence in my article about the Dearham Pottery small earthenware teapots in a later chapter.

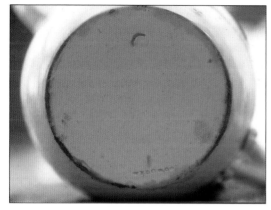

The Base.   *Double interlaced handle.*

It shows the impressed mark <u>WEDGWOOD</u>.
There is also an impressed circle on the opposite side to the mark.

Messrs Mitchells Auction Rooms in Cockermouth, West Cumbria, sold this Ester Saul teapot, in 2002. A telephone bidder started the bidding at £1,000!

In 2007 I attended the N.C.S. Summer School at Chester where Mr Tom Walford, Editor of the E.C.C. Journal showed me his most recent purchase. I was astonished to see it was the 'Susannah Drewry' inscribed creamware teapot.

When I started to write this book the details of the 2nd, 3rd and 4th creamware teapots I have noted came from three card indexes shown to me by Sheila Bidgood. However I now have details of the whereabouts of Weary Hall and its connection with the Camerton

The Susannah Drewry teapot inscribed and dated 1769.
Courtesy of Mr Tom Walford

Estates (where Aaron Wedgwood the first, and Margaret Tunstall his wife, started their married life, after leaving Whitehaven in 1704). It is situated on the right hand side of the A595 towards Carlisle, between Red Dial and Thursby, in Northern Cumbria.

According to Herbert and Mary Jackson in their book *'Camerton and Seaton, 630AD-1900'*, Christopher Curwen, second son of Christopher and Ann Porter of Weary Hall, succeeded to the Camerton Estates, West Cumberland, on the death of

The Sam Abbot and Margrett Bowman Whitehaven,
1770 inscribed and dated creamware teapot.

his brother Henry. Thomas Moule in his book *'The English Counties 1838'* records Weary Hall as the seat of Mr Charles Drewry.

Tom has very kindly given me permission to include my pictures in this volume of my book. I am certain this small teapot had been a wedding present and has never held boiling water. The Whitehaven creamware I have handled to date, is very fragile indeed, unlike the Ester Saul teapot body which is more robust and has a greyish caste to it.

The fifth teapot with a local inscription reads *Sam Abbot and Margrett Bowman Whitehaven, 1770.*

This creamware teapot has a globular body. It has chrysan-themum terminals at the end of an interlaced rope handle. It is enriched with iron red and green colours. The spout is moulded with stiff leaves to either side and it has a knob finial. It was part of the Sampson collection sale, sold on the 6th March, 1967, Lot 153.

This particular teapot appeared on the B.B.C. T.V. 'Crime Watch' programme on the 15th September, 1992, in Eric Knowles's 'Aladdin's Cave'. It was one of the many items housed in an aeroplane hanger in Knutsford mentioned previously.

The local constabulary, had been watching a man called Andrew Lewis, known as the Obituary Burglar, as he broke into the homes of recently deceased widows in Lingfield, Surrey. The police then searched his home where they found 4,000 items amongst which was the Samuel Abbot and Margrett Bowman, Whitehaven, 1770, inscribed creamware teapot.

The base of this teapot.
Photographs courtesy of Mr Eric Knowles.

This story and illustration appeared in The Daily Telegraph at the time of Andrew Lewis's conviction, photograph by kind permission of Rob. Judges, photographer, also the Daily Telegraph for permission to include the article.

A search by Anne Dick, local studies librarian, at Whitehaven Record Office revealed that the couple were married on the 16th September, 1770, at St. Bees Church, and that Samuel was in business as a Cork Cutter in Whitehaven.

No.	Proprietors	Inhabitants	Front House	Back House	Lofts	Cellar	Occupation
		1762					
		MARKET PLACE					Occupation
	Mr. Jos Gale	(Sarah Grayson	3				Spinster
		(Will Frear	7				Taylor
		(Saml. Denison			4		---
		(Robt. Gibson			4		---
		(Davd. Stalker			3		Weaver
		(Ann Murphy			1		Spinster
		(Mary Gibson			1		Do.
		(James Carny			4		---
		(Miss Peggy Gibson	2				Spinster
	Mr. Thos Gale	(-------	5				Gent
		(Richd. Pearson	8				Grocer
	Mrs. Blencowe	(Will. Reed	2				Barber
		(Richd. Brickfield			3	3	Sailor
		(John Askew	2				Taylor
		(John Douglas	5				Potter
		(Thos. Armstrong			5		Sailor
		(-------			2		---
		(Thos. Wilkinson			2		Labr.
		(John Wilson			5		Shoemr.
		(- Portis			2		Invalid
		(-------			3		---
		(Sally Cherry			3		Wido.
		(-------			1		Schoolmr.
		John Jackson	8				Apothy.
		(John Dunn	2				Stationer
		(Brid. Patinson				1	Wido.
		(Mrs. Ayles	5				Do.
		Will Shepherd	3				Printer
		Eleanor Caly				1	Wido.
		Mr. John Watts	5				Mercer
			57	–	40	5	102

1762 Whitehaven Town Census showing John Douglas, as a potter. Volume I page 19, courtesy of the Lowther family Trustees.

A cork cutting machine.

The following invoice (page 23) is for goods sent out on the ship *The Milham* in January, 1772.

The invoice not only gives us the prices but provides us with details of the type of Whitehaven pottery being shipped out to America. i.e. cream coloured ware, enamelled coffee cans etc.

On this invoice (page 24) the retailer is complaining that our Whitehaven pottery is *too fragile*. He was obviously expecting the stoneware Fulham type of pots which would withstand the rigours of a wagontrain journey, not the fragile butter pots sent out from Whitehaven then excavated in Douglas Burn (previously known as Hodgson's Croft) in 1994. (See the Andrew Pelin Map of the old Market Place; Whitehaven dated 1698 on page 15).

This following invoice (page 23) lists the various items

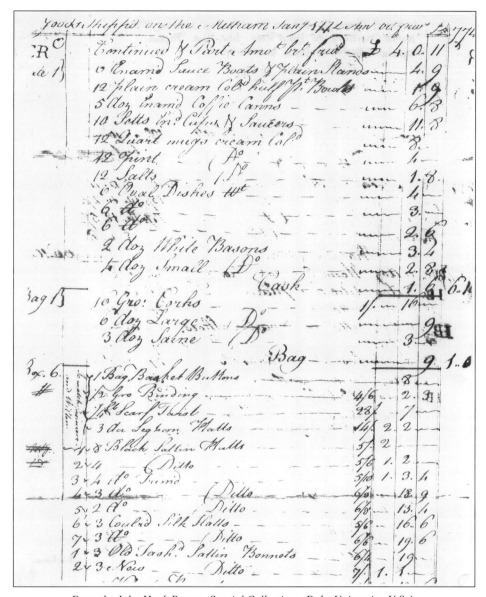

From the John Hook Papers, Special Collections, Duke University, U.S.A.

being exported from the Whitehaven Pottery in 1772 i.e. a variety of jugs, mugs, teapots, and sugar dishes, which were blue and white, enamelled and underglaze printed, in a variety of sizes.

During 1994 it was possible to excavate the area of Whitehaven Market Place shown on old maps as 'Douglas Burn'. Unfortunately I had told the owner of the site *any sign of pots come and fetch me*. I should have said *shards of pots*. Mr Christopher Cross, (the owner) told me 12 lorry loads had already gone to the tip! I had been expecting

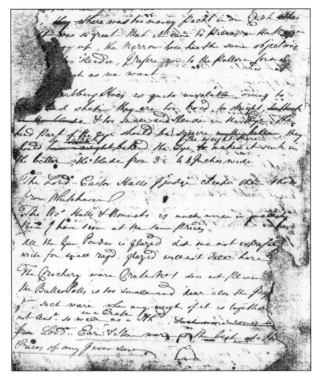

These documents were provided by Professor George L. Miller and Asst. Professor Dr. Anne Smart Martin of Winterthur University, U.S.A. These are from the John Hook papers, Business Records Collection, Virginia State Library U.S.A.

The last paragraph in the above document referring to Crate No. 1 reads 'The crockeryware crate No. 1 does not please, the Butter Pots is too small and dear also the jugs of such ware when any weight of it is together etc.'

great things from this site, as a *dressed sandstone water well* had been uncovered only days beforehand. It was only when two creamware mugs appeared, unearthed by the mechanical digger, that Christopher came running to fetch me.

The digger men on site.

The excavated creamware mugs.

The potter's water source, (his well).

Girl helpers from nearby St Bees school.

Ceramic Review December, 1971, No. 12
Gault clay-Page 7, replies to Alan Caiger Smith's letter in Issue No. 11 page 18.

Quoted from this article. 'I did not see the actual pots referred to in Alan Smith's exhibition, but I do know the Bristol and London delfts which often have pink flushes. I have always considered this to be a chrome-tin pink arising from the use of some whiting as stabiliser in the glaze. The coastal areas (would not, consider London, Bristol and Liverpool as such) often used seashells for whiting and mussel white contains some chromium. The comment on it arising from the gault clay leads me to think that the chalk in the clay contains a very small percentage (a trace really)

An 18C. kiln, Courtesy of MIKE DAVIES-SHIEL,
LANCASTER UNIVERSITY.

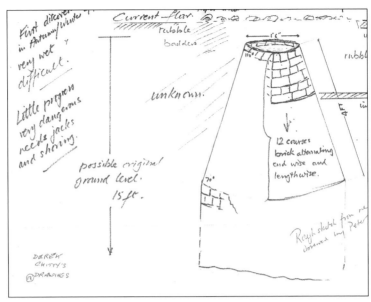

*The 'DOUGLAS BURN' kiln. Measured by MR DEREK CHITTY, Hest Bank,
also Peter Sandon and a girl pupil from nearby St. Bees, School.*

of chromium. This would account for it only flushing in harder fired ware'.

See page 27 for photograph of a box of excavated oyster shells.

**These excavations produced the following shards and pots, in both, creamware
and saltglaze.**

Small creamware vases.

A large saltglazed bowl.

Creamware plate edges (shards).

*Small unguent vases (for
ointments) and handleless tea
bowls.*

Shard of a large saltglazed bowl.

Green edged saucer shard.

Excavated tea bowls. One has a firing crack.

Boxes of shards etc., plus large oyster shells.

Washed shards. The one in the foreground is a biscuit shard.

Kiln excavations.

A young archaeologist.

Creamware sucrier. shard.

This bowl came out from within our kiln.

Various shards in creamware and saltglaze excavated in Douglas Burn.

Oyster shells.

A different shape.

Large creamware bowl.

Creamware butter pots.

Base of large bowl.

The collection of creamware illustrated below was assembled by a Whitehaven businessman, now deceased, during the 1920s and 30s. The scallop edge of the ship plate is similar to shards found during the Douglas Burn excavations.

Ale jug Success to the James and Jane.

Cordwainers Jug (shoemakers, cloggers and workers in leather).

Admiral Duncan Jug inscribed to Daniel McIntosh in the Beacon Collection.

Daniel McIntosh served under Admiral Duncan in the Battle of Campertown. He is buried in Holy Trinity Churchyard in Whitehaven. This is our oldest jug.

Temperence Lodge Whitehaven emblazoned with Masonic emblems.

Shards depicting prints of the Masonic Square and Compass

Ship plate in a private collection.

Christening Bowl made for Martin Westray, Hatter of Workington.

Martin Westray was in business as a 'Hatter' in 1794.(The Universal British Directory 1794, Page 834), C.R.O. Carlisle. In 1803 and 1805 he baptised two daughters Margaret and Mary, (Workington Church baptisms transcribed by Audrey Sykes, 1988).

CHAPTER III

NINETEENTH CENTURY
THE WHITEHAVEN POTTERY

THE WOODNORTH, HARRISON AND HALL ERA 1812-20

Local directories record that a William Cockbain described himself as a potter in the St. Bees Church parish registers when he married Abigail Borodale in 1743. In 1762 he and a man called Peter Woodnorth took over the John Douglas business, listed in the street census of Whitehaven, and were trading as Potters and Glass Dealers. In 1812 Peter Woodnorth, and new partners, leased the newly built pottery at The Ginns on the outskirts of Whitehaven from the Lowther Family. (Family correspondence courtesy of Mr Geoff Wilkinson, South Cumbria).

These men were also given permission, in 1824-5, to dig for clay from an area called The Thicket in the St. Bees Valley, an area rich in coal seams. By allowing these men to have this land and buildings the Earl of Lonsdale would be hoping to alleviate the poisonous hydrochloric acid fumes and smoke emitted by the saltglazing kiln in the Douglas Burn area (near the Market Place) which lay in a line directly in front of his Whitehaven Castle at this period of time, depending on the wind direction.

Whilst looking through the papers of the Jefferson family of Wine and Spirit Merchants in the C.R.O. Carlisle (now housed in C.R.O. Whitehaven) I came across a

Cerrusite and galena. The potter's ores, courtesy of R. and J. Bennett, Distington Cumbria.

letter from a Sailor in Antigua to his parents in Whitehaven which read *'I'm sorry to hear of your indisposition still continuing, as I have already said, I expect nothing else, whilst you still continue in that smoking hole'*. The date of the letter 1781.

One of Peter Woodnorth's partners, thought to be his financial backer, was a Mr John Harrison, a rich Whitehaven Merchant with interests in brewing, banking, rope making, and shipping and trade with Virginia. A sleeping partner was Mr John Tebay of the Keswick Mines which produced the ores necessary in the glazing process of pottery manufacture i.e. cerrusite, galena etc.

In an advertisement in the Isle of Man Gazette on the 14th January, 1814.

W.I.RYDER,
DEALER IN GLASS, CHINA AND EARTHENWARE

Informs his friends and the public that he has lately imported a quantity of goods consisting of the under mentioned articles:-

Blue and White	Table services complete
Brown Lined	Table services complete
Blue and Green Grass Edged	Table services complete
Tea Services Complete - Various Patterns	
Jugs, Ewers, and Basins	
Wine Coolers	
Vases for Chimney Ornaments	
Silver Lustre Sugar and Cream Ewers	
Egyptian Black	

Sets of China, Table Services from the Manufactory at the shortest notice. Coarse Black Ware of all descriptions, and Stone Jars from half a gallon to five gallons

Hampers or crates carefully packed and sent away to any part of the Island. Shops or Hawkers supplied at the *Whitehaven Prices.*

This list of items provides us with the most comprehensive view available of the sort of wares made at the Whitehaven Pottery in the early 19th century.

In May, 1819 the following advertisement was published in the *Cumberland Pacquet* Newspaper, on behalf of the Whitehaven Pottery.

WOODNORTH, Harrison and Hall and Co., Manufacturers of earthenware viz. of blue printed, blue painted, blue and green edged, fine and common cream colour, black, purple, red and rose coloured, printed, and a great variety of fancy coloured ware, figured and embossed ware:- beg leave to inform the public in general that they have opened a warehouse, No. 10, in the Market Place, where Housekeepers and others may be supplied with the above descriptions of wares, of a quality equal, if not superior, to the generality of Staffordshire ware, and at much lower prices than Staffordshire ware of the same quality, can possibly be sold at. (*see N.C.S. 'Echoes and Reflections'* published in 1990, page 43, by Elizabeth Adams).

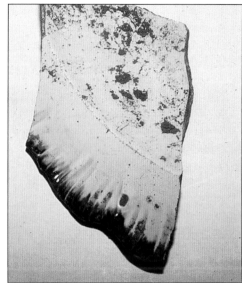

Blue and green grass (shell edged) shards.

Blue edged shard.

The pots of this era are very rare, but of sound quality for this period in the history of British ceramics.

To date I have recorded two identical pearlware dinner plates which are inscribed 'R D' in the centre. They are both underglaze decorated in cobalt blue. One is impressed on the reverse Woodnorth and Co., whilst the other reads W. and Co., which is remarkable

THE 2 R.D. INSCRIBED PEARLWARE PLATES.
These photographs show the workman's mark, in cobalt blue, (top right) which is identical to the workman's mark recorded on the Whitehaven Pottery Nanking patterned jugs.
(Courtesy of Barbara Blenkinship and Beatrice Stocks).

as they depict an identical print and inscription. One has a 4 inch body crack, but both are wonderful survivors for nearly 2 centuries.

The plates display the same border as the Lowther patterned plate (see photograph in chapter referring to Dinnerware). this plate also depicts the impressed factory mark W. & Co. on the reverse.

Amongst my documents and the Whitehaven factory pots recorded to date, it is noticeable that many refer to members of the Dixon family of Whitehaven the most important being Mary Dixon, wife of Aaron Wedgwood III. I wonder is the potter recorded in the St. Bees Church registers Mary's brother, and, as Aaron was working for Peter How at Low Mill (which is located nearby), did he give his brother in law a job?

1767	St. Bees Church Registers record John Dixon, Potter
1812-20	The two pearlware plates inscribed R.D., are marked, and are of the Whitehaven pottery James Brindley (Engraver) era.
1830	An initialled W.D. loving cup which is underglaze transfer printed in a palette of mauve and green.
1851	A blue and white tobacco jar which is signed underneath S.D. and dated 1851 and is inscribed by Sarah Dixon.

Sarah was the grandmother of Mr Charles Humphreys, Chief Mining Surveyor for the West Cumberland Coalfield, (in the 1950s). The family lived on Meadow View then moved to High Street, Whitehaven. Fortunately his widow allowed me to photograph the family pots in the 1980s. After I had photographed them Mrs Humphreys senior presented her inscribed tobacco jar by Sarah Dixon to the Whitehaven Museum. Their son Charles junior

The Sarah Dixon tobacco jar. The tobacco jar on the top reads 'to John Corlett by doter Jane aged 16 1851'.

The W.D. initialled loving cup which I had been allowed to photograph by Mrs Humphreys senior, some years previously.

The potters had their own idiosyncratic manner of spelling by phonetic means e.g. doter.

inherited these family pots, however he died prematurely.

The pots were sent to Messrs. Mitchells Auctioneers, Cockermouth, where the small family commemorative Coronation Mug (these had been inscribed for the pupils of the Glass House School in Whitehaven) fetched more than £850.

Fortunately other Whitehaven families had given their mugs to the Museum in Whitehaven. These form part of the the Beacon Collection.

Woodnorth and Harrison invited the Staffordshire Potter John Hall of Messrs John Hall and Sons, Burslem, Stafffordshire to join them in this new venture, i.e. the Whitehaven Pottery. Hall in turn persuaded the engraver James Brindley, living at this time (1818) at No.18, Union Buildings in Staffordshire to come to work for the Whitehaven Pottery.

It was James Brindley who signed and dated the first recorded Whitehaven plate, (printed in monochrome and recorded by Dr. Geoffrey Godden in the Appendix of his *Encyclopaedia of British Pottery and Porcelain Marks, Page 736 Item 4515)*. Dr. Godden records 'this plate is impressed Woodnorth and Co., and is dated on the milestone **1819** and signed James Brindley, within the grass, in the foreground. The drawing on this plate is 1 of a set of 12 commissioned from the artist Havelock, Knight and Brown, "Phiz" of *Punch* and illustrator of *Dickens*, by the ceramics firm William Brownfield, Corbridge, Staffordshire'. He goes on to record 'it is not known how the Whitehaven Pottery obtained this engraving but it was not registered for patent'.

The James Brindley signed plate.

The plate, recorded by Dr. Godden, was said to have been housed in the Bethnal Green Museum, London, now the Museum of Childhood He records *'a plate fitting this description was sold by Messrs. Sotheby's in l955'*. I have made many enquiries to the various Museum Services regarding the whereabouts of this very important early Whitehaven Pottery plate, to no avail.

This plate is certainly proof that the Staffordshire engraver was working for the Whitehaven Pottery in 1819. E. Morton Nance, author of *The Manufacture of Porcelain at Swansea and Nantgarw* Appendix IX, p.539, records 'According to Turner, James Brindley visited Swansea at different times but recorded his earliest engagement here to be 1835-45 and coming again about 1852'.*

Peter Woodnorth's partner, John Hall, of Messrs John Hall and Sons, Burslem, Staffordshire, was declared bankrupt in 1832. James Brindley left Whitehaven shortly after and found work at the Glamorgan Pottery. According to a report in the *Staffordshire Advertiser*, 1795-1865 John Hall's effects were auctioned lst June, 1833 and the estate finally settled 19th May, 1838'. (Courtesy of Rodney Hampson, published by the N.C.S. in 2000.)

John Hall was aged 76 when he died on the lst, September, 1838, whilst living with his daughter and son-in-law, Mary and John Wilkinson, the then owners of the Whitehaven Pottery.

Helen Hallesey, author of the book *The Glamorgan Pottery* and I have been in communication with regards to James Brindley's work both in Whitehaven and at the Glamorgan Pottery, Swansea, Wales.

The evidence from shards, excavated here in Whitehaven by the author, and two nearly identical saucers, one discovered locally, the second in George Haggerty's shop in the Grass Market, Edinburgh, (see picture below) has enabled Helen and I to record the differences in his work. We now realise James Brindley must have taken some of the Whitehaven copper plates to the Glamorgan Pottery, altering them slightly. The differences were reported in our N.C.S Newsletter No. 132, December, 2003 Page 8.

The two saucers plus wasters (one in biscuit).
Helen Hallesy has named this pattern 'Mandarin with long pipe'.

These two early 19th century saucers are unique. The brown and white saucer was made at the Whitehaven Pottery, whilst the blue and white one was made at the Glamorgan Pottery, in Wales. Note the unglazed biscuit shard of an egg cup with the pattern printed on, centre left, also the pale blue saucer shards from the Whitehaven Pottery site, whilst the Welsh saucer shows a darker blue colour.

Ceramics expert Robert Copeland reckons 'flow-blue' was achieved by accident

---

* *(Courtesy of Mr Derek Chitty, Hest Bank).*

due to the potter's inadequate knowledge of chemistry. The various colours of blue are recorded in his book Spode's Willow Pattern on the manufacturing process Chapter 3 – Cobalt Blue.

*Late in the eighteenth century the development of a Press by Needham and Kite saw the extraction of excess water from clay also the introduction of magnets to rid the clay of any particles of iron which stained it.

At the beginning of the nineteenth century a Flint Mill was built in Whitehaven to crush flints. The men working in the Flint Mill developed Pneumoconiosis and many finished in an early grave as their lungs rotted from inhaling the dust in the crushing process.

Clay and coal were in plentiful supply in the Ginns area so the Whitehaven potter Peter Woodnorth recruited two partners, one a Banker and one a Staffordshire man (a master Potter). He hired skilled workmen, artists and engravers, everything was now ready for the production of pottery.

They even attempted to make soft paste porcelain. This consists of a pliable *plastic ball clay and other glassy materials* but it proved an expensive process, one which the parochial potteries could ill afford. 'Ball clay' is washed out from cliffs and quarries with high powered water hoses these days, sometimes in balls weighing approximately 40lbs or more and usually found around Dartmoor in Devon.

China clay (or red marl) is mined in Cornwall and burns white when fired. It consists of rotting felspar which has been under the ground for thousands of years and china clay is the final decomposition. The clay is solid, not pliable like the ball clay. When one sees 'Stone China' on the reverse of a large ashet it tells us the body is more robust and will stand more wear and tear than pots made from ball clay.

The early nineteenth century industrial chemists experimented to try to produce enamel colours, they used chrome and discovered it would stand the high temperatures used in the underglaze decoration process. Chrome produced a range of greens as illustrated on page 31, which shows the 'grass' coloured shell edged shards of plates, also the blobbing in a vivid *green enamel of the daisy moulded borders* of shards and whole plates in the 'Children's Plates' section on page 116. Using a mixture of tin oxide they later produced the colour pink as illustrated on a Child's plate 'Begger's Petition' on page 118. Peter Woodnorth's brother Joseph was a partner in the firm of 'Woodnorth and Wilson', Chemists of Whitehaven at this period.

It has been recorded that in the middle of the nineteenth century the potters started to use *calcined ox bones* in the manufacture of their pots. Seemingly small jars were made using a *paste of calcined ox bone ash* which was then shaped round the inside of a mould then left to dry out. When ready they were lead glazed and fired in a kiln to harden off. In an Assay Office the Assay Officer could now pour his melted gold/silver into one of these small jars in order to weigh it accurately thus began our knowledge of the manufacture of Bone China!

---

*   *This information was gleaned from papers sent to me by M. and N. Davies Shiel of Lancaster University.*

Author with Ester Saul Teapot.

Small creamware mug.

Kiln Furniture.

Banded ware.

The reverse of the willow pattern shards read 'Stone China' Semi China (with an impressed star).

A small 'Sealeaf pattern' milk jug.

A truly wonderful object made by the Whitehaven Pottery at this era 1812-20 is the Hillis Bowl. (Recorded in the N.C.S. Newsletter No. 38, June, 1980).

It is decorated with underglaze black prints that have been further enriched with high temperature colours in a Pratt palette of blue, green, yellow and orange. The main print which decorates the interior of the bowl shows a large country mansion with a

THE HILLIS BOWL
17.5 inches across, 7.5 inches high, and has a 10 inch base.
(Photograph of the "Hillis Bowl" courtesy of Dr. Maurice and
Lyn Hillis).

church on the left. In the foreground is a river beside which stroll a lady and gentleman watching two gentlemen fishing on the opposite bank, while a young child and a dog play by the couple's side. This print is also arranged around the exterior wall of the bowl. The interior wall is decorated with a hunting scene of riders and hounds while the rim bears an elaborate flared design with reserved cartouches in which are placed cows and sheep. The foot is also decorated with a similar design but the cartouches contain hunting and coursing scenes. The total effect is of elaboration and richness but it is nevertheless very attractive. The factory mark W.H.H.WHITEHAVEN is under-glaze printed in black, on the base of the bowl.

I have recorded two dinner plates depicting the same scene as the Hillis Bowl however neither has a pattern name; I have therefore christened the pattern Lowther.

The part factory mark (not in the picture) reads
W.H.H. WHITEHAVEN. It also has a flared rim.
It depicts Whitehaven Castle and shows two horses
grazing on the front lawn.

The interior of the Hillis Bowl.

This salt-glazed and moulded tobacco jar is owned by Jean Sanders of Whitehaven. I am fairly certain this was made in Whitehaven 'Do you Ken John Peel' being the County anthem.

Man in a white shirt with hay fork.

Shards of delft. On the tiny shard (centre), a man can be seen with a hay fork. (See picture on the left)

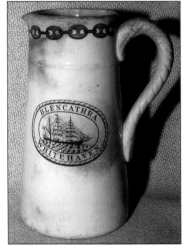

Stoneware Ship's Jug, printed with the Whitehaven Ship 'The Blencathra.' It is also the name of a Cumbrian mountain).

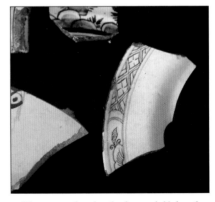

These are shards of a large delft bowl.

These dinner plates are of an earthenware body and are underglaze transfer printed in blue/white. The border of one is identical to that on the pair of recently discovered pearlware plates inscribed R.D. one of which is impressed W. & Co., whilst the other has neither a border nor a mark. However the author has in her collection another early

Two Lowther pattern plates, the one on the left is a sheet pattern.

Plate on the right "with border" is impressed W. & Co.

The master mould showing a hunting scene which is impressed on the bottom edge WOODNORTH & Co. as depicted on the Water set on the right.

Soft paste, beaker and water jug blue sprigged, Beacon Collection, Whitehaven. Two of our oldest pots.

Whitehaven Pottery, blue and white dinner plate underglaze transfer printed which also has no border, but has the factory mark with the pattern name The Minstrel. (See photograph in the later chapter on Dinner wares).

In 2001 my husband purchased this Master Mould which was being auctioned at Messrs Mitchells Auction Co., Cockermouth. A huntsman is shown climbing over a fence accompanied by his hounds. WOODNORTH & Co. is impressed on the bottom edge of the mould.

The Wilkinson family correspondence gives details of how two young men, (sons of well known Staffordshire potting families) sailed to the U.S.A. in 1820.

One was John Wilkinson junior, who sought clay suitable for the manufacture of pottery or porcelain, whilst his friend John Hall junior, sought business potential for trade with America, (to be Agent for his father John Hall of the Staffordshire potteries, and perhaps the Whitehaven Pottery?).

The *Boston Almanac and Business Directory 1875,* under Crockery, Page 223 records a John Hall still trading in 1875. His premises being 7, Doane Street, Boston, USA. (Courtesy of Mr and Mrs Rodney Hampson, Staffs).

The family correspondence states John Wilkinson junior did not discover deposits of clay suitable for the manufacture of pots and returned to England in 1822.

Two years later, a Staffordshire church marriage register for 1824 records John Wilkinson had married Mary Hall, daughter of John Hall Senior (a partner in the Whitehaven Pottery). Mary and John moved to Whitehaven and took over the lease of the Whitehaven Pottery from Peter Woodnorth and Co.

The Verriville Pottery at Finniston, Scotland in 1836 showing the large chimney, (a record at that period in time,) 120' high and used for the production of cut glass. Colonel John Geddes' house and gardens can be seen on the left of the picture. From a sketch by the late Mr Andrew Macgeorge.

That same year Eliza the 17 year old daughter of Peter Woodnorth died, so he decided to leave Whitehaven and take over the management of the Verriville Pottery, Glasgow, Scotland.

On the 21st, November, 1828 an indenture of assignment was deposited at the office of Solicitors Wilson and Perry of Whitehaven, recording that everything was to be transferred to Joseph Woodnorth (presumably a son who stayed in Whitehaven) and William Wilson to pay all creditors. William Wilson was a Chemist*, (a partner in the Whitehaven firm Wilson and Kitchin). (Kitchin being a name associated with the oldest of the Whitehaven potteries, the Ginns House).

In 1830 Mr Geddes the owner of the Verriville Pottery had leased it to a Mr Montgomery who took as his principal assistant and sales representative Mr Peter Woodnorth. Woodnorth set out reorganising the works, spending £500 on this aspect. In 1831 the two partners purchased the warehouse at Greenock which had belonged to Geddes and the following year two more warehouses in Waterford and Limerick, Eire. Unfortunately two of their ships, full of Verriville Pottery, sank (*the Hope and the Helena*) in 1832 and 1833 respectively, before they reached Limerick.

In the Whitehaven Cemetery a Memorial on a tombstone reads as follows:-
In affectionate remembrance of Peter Woodnorth formerly of this town who died 4th February 1856 aged 46 years also Hannah his wife who died 12th June, 1854 aged 42 years, both were interred at St. Paul's Church, Burslem, Staffordshire also Robert their son who died 12th November, 1917 aged 67 years, Elizabeth wife of Robert Woodnorth died in Hamilton, Canada 23rd April, 1936 aged 86years, Peter Woodnorth son of Robert and Elizabeth who died 26th April, 1934 aged 49 years of age.

WHITEHAVEN POTTERY
The John and Mary Wilkinson Era, 1820-1867.

The evidence of factory marks, for this period in the life of the Whitehaven pottery, proves that the Woodnorth, Harrison and Hall partnership had appointed John Wilkinson (John Hall's future son-in-law) to be the manager of the Whitehaven pottery before they sent him and John Hall Junior to the U.S.A. in 1820.

Dr. Geoffrey Godden, (expert on ceramics), has stated in many of his lectures and books that 'before 1820 all potters and clockmakers signed their work 'I' be they James, John or Joseph (as there was no 'J' in the Roman Alphabet)'.

The factory marks on the Whitehaven pottery wares before 1820 read W.H.H., W. & Co., and WOODNORTH & Co. With the change in management in 1822 the initials I.W. are then underglaze printed on the factory pots (John Wilkinson).

From 1824 until he retired in 1867 the Whitehaven Pottery marks read J.W. plus the pattern name, usually within a cartouche. A second mark shows a description of the ware being included in the factory mark i.e. Warranted Stone China, or Semi-

---

* *(courtesy of Anne Dick, Whitehaven).*

China, with the initials J.W. underneath. A third marks reads JOHN WILKINSON, WHITEHAVEN.

The photograph on the right proves the Wilkinson family were not alone in their search for suitable clay for pottery and porcelain in America.

Mary and John Wilkinson brought Randle Wilkinson (their nephew), from Brownhills, Staffordshire (presumably the son of John's brother). (These facts are recorded on the census returns for Whitehaven, dated 1851 C.R.O Whitehaven). It also states that John Wilkinson originated from Tunstall, Staffordshire. As a grown man Randle (named after his grandfather in Staffordshire) trained to become the Company Accountant for the Whitehaven Pottery.

When John Wilkinson died in 1868, Randle, (still living with his Auntie Mary) took over the day to day running of the pottery for the next nine years. It was no wonder Mary left it to him in her will when she died in 1877. When eldest son George

This photograph of a plaque erected at quarry No. 36 West Mills, Nr Franklin, South Carolina, U.S.A, was taken by Sally Connor, Whitehaven, in 2005. It proves other potters had been taking clay from the U.S.A., the date 1767.

John and Mary Wilkinson.   *(Courtesy of Geoff Wilkinson).*

Descendants of Randle Wilkinson 1726-1821.
The Wilkinson Family Tree

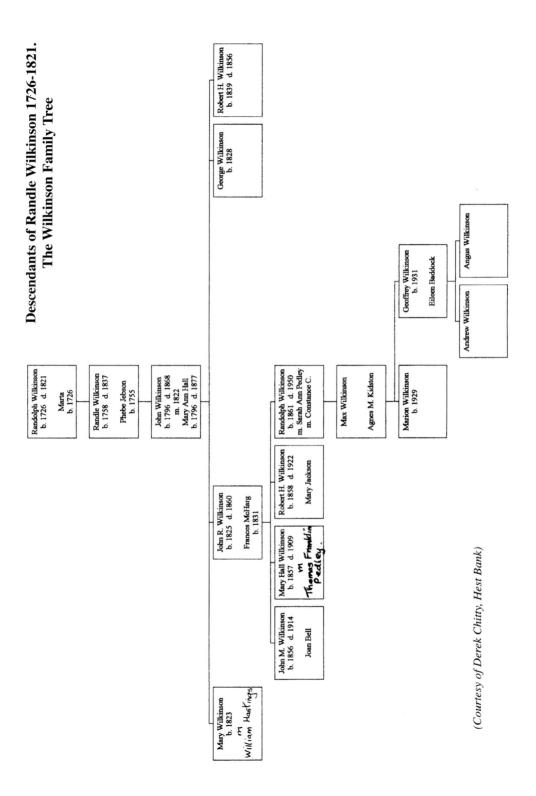

Randolph Wilkinson
b. 1726 d. 1821

Marta
b. 1726

Randle Wilkinson
b. 1758 d. 1837

Phebe Jebson
b. 1755

John Wilkinson
b. 1796 d. 1868
m. 1822
Mary Ann Hall
b. 1796 d. 1877

George Wilkinson
b. 1828

Robert H. Wilkinson
b. 1839 d. 1856

Mary Wilkinson
b. 1823
m
William Hastings

John R. Wilkinson
b. 1825 d. 1860

Frances McHarg
b. 1831

John M. Wilkinson
b. 1856 d. 1914

Joan Bell

Mary Hall Wilkinson
b. 1857 d. 1909
m
Thomas Franklin Pedley.

Robert H. Wilkinson
b. 1858 d. 1922

Mary Jackson

Randolph Wilkinson
b. 1861 d. 1950
m. Sarah Ann Pedley
m. Constance C.

Max Wilkinson

Agnes M. Kidston

Marion Wilkinson
b. 1929

Geoffrey Wilkinson
b. 1931

Eileen Baddock

Andrew Wilkinson

Angus Wilkinson

(Courtesy of Derek Chitty, Hest Bank)

(trading as a Draper in the town), signed his father's death certificate, (as a witness) the address he gave was 'Woodbine Villas', Meadow View, Whitehaven.

It was the son George, (on behalf of the rest of the family), who contested Mary's will. The outcome of the case resulted in the pottery having to be sold. Litigation costs swallowed up nearly all the money, and according to the family correspondence, Geoff Wilkinson's grandfather states he received only £3 10s. The correspondence goes on to record that son George then emigrated to the U.S.A.

The family letters, which follow, prove the connection between the Wilkinson family of potters and at least five other well known pottery factories throughout Great Britain, namely.

1. His g.g.g.g. Grandfather RANDLE WILKINSON is said to have worked for MINTON'S, in fact one of the Mintons was an executor to his will.

2. His g.g.g. Grandfather JOHN WILKINSON owned the WHITEHAVEN POTTERY

3. His g.g.g. Grandmother MARY WILKINSON (John's wife) was the daughter of MR JOHN HALL, of MESSRS JOHN HALL and SONS, BURSLEM, STAFFORDSHIRE.

4. MAX WILKINSON, (Geoff's father) married AGNES M. KITSON daughter of ROBERT and MARY ANN KITSON.

5. ROBERT KITSON owned the VERRIVILLE and ANDERSTON POTTERIES, GLASGOW, SCOTLAND.

6. ROBERT KITSON'S WIFE, MARY ANN, was the daughter of MR JOB MEIGH, of HANLEY, STAFFORDSHIRE.

Geoff Wilkinson and Linda Kohlstamm .g.g.grandchildren of John and Mary Wilkinson, outside the Beacon, Whitehaven in 2005. Linda Kohstamm lives in Seattle, U.S.A. Her g. grandfather being George son of John Wilkinson.

Henry Kelly, author of the book *Scottish Ceramics* page 187, records Robert Kitson taking control of the Verriville Pottery. Ironically this is the same pottery which Peter Woodnorth, (a founder member of the Whitehaven Pottery) managed, until he and Montgomery went bankrupt in 1833. Robert Kitson also owned the Anderston Pottery and Glassworks, near Glasgow, Scotland.

Whitehaven Pottery made and sold a lot of creamware in the early 19th century. It

Bryanston Hindhead Surrey 10 Jan. 1943.

My dear Max — my father

In your last letter you ask if I can tell you much about my ancestors. Unfortunately when I was young I did not take any particular interest in my predecessors else I might have derived much interesting information from my grandmother who died at 80 when I was 16. She was a Hall from the Staffordshire Pottery District & was connected in some way with Robert Hall an outstanding Baptist Minister in middle of 18th century; about 1757 or thereabouts. The Wilkinsons were of a Cheshire family bordering on Staffordshire — My grandfather was in early years associated with Mintons Pottery whose ware was very noted; & one of the Mintons was an executor of my grandfathers will — My grandfather went to the USA early on in his career with the idea of starting a pottery business there but found the difficulties at that time of finding the right kind of clay insuperable so he returned to England & in 1842 took over the Whitehaven Pottery from its first owners (established 1816) & carried it on in his own name until his death in 1868 & my grandmother kept it going until her death 9 years later The estate was thrown into Chancery & was swallowed up in legal costs — My share should have been about £1200 but I actually only received £5–10.0!! When my grandfather went to the USA his brother in law John Hall accompanied him but he remained & established a large business in imported earthenware from Staffordshire & this was still carried on by his son in Boston when I visited him in May 1892 & for all I know is still in existence — The Wilkinson forbears are buried in some churchyard at Sandbach & Barthomley in Cheshire — Some of the Pedleys married into Hall families & your mother Jenny Talby's mother's maiden name was Pedley — Granny Allen on her honeymoon went to Whitehaven & stayed with my grandmother & the latter wrote to her later on congratulating her on the birth of a daughter that is on your grandmother Lois' arrival.

Wilkinson family correspondence.
                    (Courtesy of Mr Geoff Wilkinson, South Cumbria).

The John Wilkinson you ask about was some connection of our family – not very near I believe – I once had a copper coin token of John Wilkinson, Ironmaster on it & an engraving of an anvil on one side – It was dated 1780 or so I think – I gave it to John many years ago – I was the same John Wilkinson who built the first iron boat. I saw it safely afloat at Lindal in Cartmel the Furness District of North Lancashire The whole countryside turned out to see his folly & the vessel sank & did went away confounded – He also made cast iron pipes & some of these were converted into cannon at the French Revolution – I think I have now told you all I know & am sorry it cannot be more exact

I shall probably be in Glasgow for our Meetings on 25th Jany so unless you hear to contrary I shall hope to lunch with you & you dine with me as usual

With love from your affectionate Father

Randolph Wilkinson

P.S. The Wilkinson of Burslem may have been the same as above John Wilkinson, at the Ironmaster had a foundry somewhere in Western part of Midland counties – Tunstall one of the Staffs Pottery towns has a Wilkinson Street in it & Randle Wilkinsons parents once resided there

Wilkinson family correspondence.
(Courtesy of Mr Geoff Wilkinson, South Cumbria).

Linda and her husband Ed., Craig Hutchinson, (late Collections Officer, the Beacon), Mr Tom Scott, a researcher, and the Author, outside The Beacon, Whitehaven. Whitehaven Harbour is in the background.

was cheaper to produce than the soft-paste porcelain which required a high temperature and therefore was costly on fuel. Printing and painting was expensive. The master engravers were Sadler and Green of Liverpool who worked exclusively for the great Josiah Wedgwood in Staffordshire, producing exquisite creamware or Queens Ware as it became known. It is no wonder Catherine the Great of Russia ordered the famous Frog Service from them.

However later excavations on the Whitehaven pottery site produced shards of fine creamware see page 36.

 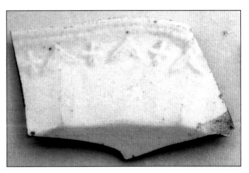

The shards illustrated above show
1. a triple daisy moulded border.
2. dimpled florets.
3. a small single daisy moulded border.

This shard is of a plate border, the outer rim shows rouletted impressed dots whilst the inner border rim shows alternating inverted Vs and small '+'. See Fig.4 N.C.S. Newsletter No. 112 Dec., 1998, page 9.

These and others were excavated on the Whitehaven pottery site. (Courtesy of the owners of the site Mr and Mrs Tom Mossop).

John Wilkinson's foreman potter was Mr Brown Harrison who lived in Howgill Street, Whitehaven. The following photograph shows his large imposing headstone which proves the affection and esteem with which John Wilkinson held this foreman.

 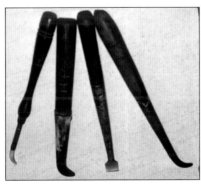 

Potters tools.
Courtesy of Wendy Mitton, Carlisle.

This is the funeral sheet for John Wilkinson's funeral.
Courtesy of Michael Moon, Antiquarian Book Seller, Lowther Street, Whitehaven, Cumbria.

The Whitehaven Pottery (The White Pottery).

Undoubtedly the 1820-40 period was the heyday of The Whitehaven Pottery. The quality of their products being equal to the Scottish, Welsh and Staffordshire potteries.

The following are records from a customs document referring to a ship load of earthenware and creamware despatched to Maitland Kennedy and Co., Philadelphia, U.S.A. The wares were purchased by a John Dawson from Mr John Wilkinson, Whitehaven Pottery. The document is dated 10th March, 1836 and refers to 40 crates of earthenware, 15 tons of coal, 120 tons of common salt and 30 tons of stored salt. (courtesy of Prof. George Miller and Asst. Prof. Dr Anne Smart-Martin, Wintherthur University, U.S.A).

CUSTOMS DOCUMENT

	£	s	d
It records the overall price:-	349	17	03
Crates, straw and cartage	17	13	04
	367	10	07

The cost of the crates of earthenware as listed on the customs declaration is £238 18s 1d. This suggests a 35% discount from the Whitehaven Pottery. This is a typical discount for the mid 1830s period.

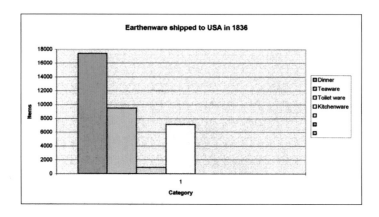

from research on "The Market Basket of Ceramics
typically available in Country Stores from 1700 to 1900"
George L. Miller
University of Delaware
Center for Archaeological Research, Dept of Anthropology
Newark, Del. *19*

Summary of the Whitehaven invoice, March 10, 1836

This invoice is an uncataloged document in the Collection of Business Americana of the Smithsonian Institution, Museum of National History.

The wares were purchased by John Dawson from John Wilkinson, Whitehaven Pottery, on 26th of February, 1836, the invoice is for 40 crates of ceramics which was summarized as follows:

```
                                    L 349/17/3
        crates, straw and cartage     17/13/4
                                    -----------
                                    L 367/10/7
```

This invoice is attached to the Customs declaration that was made on March 10th of 1836 which also included 15 tons of coal, 120 tons of common salt, and 30 tons of "stored" salt. In this declaration the 40 crates of earthenware were listed at L 238/81/1 which suggest a 35 percent discount from the Whitehaven pottery. That is a typical discount rate for the mid-1830s.

Thirty-one of the crates of earthenware were assorted for the country trade. The other nine were made up of table and kitchen wares. Together they contained 34,955 vessels which at the list price cost 2.4 English pence each. After the discount, their cost averaged 1.64 English pence each. Taking the English pound at an exchange rate of $4.80, the average wholesale cost of these vessels in Liverpool was 3.28 cents American.

The breakdown of the Assorted crates is as follows:

TEA WARE	9,485	33.00%
TABLEWARE	12,464	43.36%
KITCHEN WARE	6,040	21.01%
TOILET WARE	756	2.63%
	-------	-------
	28,745	100.00

The remaining nine crates had the following breakdown:

TABLEWARE	4,938	79.51%
KITCHEN WARE	1,112	17.91%
TOILET WARE	160	2.58%
	-------	-------
	6,210	100.00

The assorted crates averaged 927 vessels, while the others averaged 690 vessels.

1836 CRATES ASSORTED OF CERAMICS

40 crates from the Whitehaven Pottery shipped to Maitland Kennedy Co. of Philadelphia March 26, 1836.

5 crates, numbered 1 through 5

TEA WARE	CC	EDG	DIPT	PAI	PRI	LET	total
teas unh			180				180
teas hnd					144		144
Irish teas hnd					36		36
tea pots					8		8
creams				12	4		16
cream ewers					6		6
sugars							
	---	---	---	---	---	---	---
tea				192	198		390

DINNER WARE	CC	EDG	DIPT	PAI	PRI	LET	total
dishes		8			8		16
plates	36	48			48		132
twiflers	36	72			48		156
muffins		72			48	72	192
bakers					6		6
nappies		8					8
	---	---	---	---	---	---	---
table	72	208			158	72	510

KITCHEN WARE	CC	EDG	DIPT	PAI	PRI	LET	total
bowls	30		30		28		88
jugs					12		12
mugs	24		24			24	72
	---	---	---	---	---	---	---
kitchen	54		54		40	24	172

TOILET WARE	CC	EDG	DIPT	PAI	PRI	LET	total
ewers							
basins	6						6
chambers	12						12
	---	---	---	---	---	---	---
toilet	18						18

	CC	EDG	DIPT	PAI	PRI	LETTERED	total	%
tea				192	198		390	35.78
table	72	208			158	72	510	46.79
kitchen	54		54		40	24	172	15.78
toilet	18						18	1.65
	---	---	---	---	---	---	---	------
	144	208	54	192	468	24	1,090	100.00

6 crates numbered 15 through 20, Whitehaven Pottery, 1836

TEA WARE	CC	EDG	DIPT	PAI	PRI	WIL	BROS	LET	total
tea sets unh				216	144				360
tea sets hnd						36			36
Irish, hnd					8				8
coffee pots					8				8
creams			12	4					16
sugars									
	---	---	---	---	---	---	---	---	---
tea				228	156		36		420

DINNER WARE	CC	EDG	DIPT	PAI	PRI	WIL	BROS	LET	total
dishes		8			8				16
plates		48			48				96
twiflers		72			48				120
muffins		72			48			72	192
bakers					6				6
nappies									
salts		12							12
	---	---	---	---	---	---	---	---	---
table		212			158			72	442

KITCHEN WARE	CC	EDG	DIPT	PAI	PRI	WIL	BROS	LET	total
bowls	24		30		28				82
jugs	12				12				24
mugs/cans	21		15					18	54
	---	---	---	---	---	---	---	---	---
kitchen	57		45		40			18	160

TOILET WARE	CC	EDG	DIPT	PAI	PRI	WIL	BROS	LET	total
ewers									
hand basins	6								6
chambers	12								12
	---	---	---	---	---	---	---	---	---
toilet	18								18

	CC	EDG	DIPT	PAI	PRI	WIL	BROS	LET	total	%
tea				228	156		36		420	40.38
table		212			158			72	442	42.50
kitchen	57		45		40			18	160	15.38
toilet	18								18	1.73
	---	---	---	---	---	---	---	---	---	------
	75	212	45	300	214	158	36		1,040	99.99

4 crates numbered 21 through 24, Whitehaven Pottery, 1836

TEA WARE	CC	EDG	DIPT	PAI	PRI	WILL	LET	total
tea sets unh				144				144
tea sets hnd					72			72
tea pots					3			3
creams			6	2				8
sugars								
	---	---	---	---	---	---	---	---
tea				150	77			227

DINNER WARE	CC	EDG	DIPT	PAI	PRI	WILL	LET	total
dishes		4			6			10
plates	24	36			24			84
twiflers	36	48			12			96
muffins					24	36		60
bakers					3			3
nappies	12							12
turtles		6						6
salts		12						12
butters tubs					2			2
	---	---	---	---	---	---	---	---
table	72	106			2	69	36	285

KITCHEN WARE	CC	EDG	DIPT	PAI	PRI	WILL	LET	total
bowls		72	30	8				110
jugs	6				14			20
mugs	18		22				12	52
	---	---	---	---	---	---	---	---
kitchen	24		94	30	22		12	182

TOILET WARE	CC	EDG	DIPT	PAI	PRI	WILL	LET	total
ewers	2				1			3
basins	2				1			3
chambers	5				1			6
	---	---	---	---	---	---	---	---
toilet	9				3			12

	CC	EDG	DIPT	PAI	PRI	WILL	LETTER	total	%
tea				150	77			227	32.15
table	72	106			2	69	36	285	40.37
kitchen	24		94	30	22		12	182	25.78
toilet	9				3			12	1.70
	---	---	---	---	---	---	---	---	------
	105	106	94	180	104	69	48	706	100.00

1 crate, number 25, Whitehaven Pottery, 1836

	CC	EDG	DIPT	PAI	PRI	WILL	LET	total
TEA WARE								
tea sets unh				144				144
tea sets hnd					72			72
tea pots					3			3
creams				6	2			8
sugars								
tea				150	77			227
DINNER WARE								
dishes		4			6			10
plates	24	36			24			84
twiflers	36	48			12			96
muffins					24	36		60
bakers					3			3
nappies	12							12
turtles		6						6
salts		12						12
butters tubs				2				2
table	72	106		2	69	36		285

	CC	EDG	DIPT	PAI	PRI	WILL	LET	total
KITCHEN WARE								
bowls			72	30	8			110
jugs	6				14			20
mugs	12		18				12	42
kitchen	18		90	30	22		12	172
TOILET WARE								
ewers	2				1			3
basins	2				1			3
chambers	5				1			6
toilet	9				3			12

	CC	EDG	DIPT	PAI	PRI	WILL	LETTER	total	%
tea				150	77			227	32.61
table	72	106		2	69	36		285	40.95
kitchen	18		90	30	22		12	172	24.71
toilet	9				3			12	1.72
	99	106	90	180	104	69	48	696	99.99

2 crates, numbers 26 and 27, Whitehaven Pottery, 1836

	CC	EDG	DIPT	PAI	PRI	WILL	JAPAN	total
TEA WARE								
teas unh				216				216
teas hnd								
Irish teas, hnd				24				24
bowls & saucer hnd				12				12
tea pots								
creams								
sugars								
tea				252				252
DINNER WARE								
dishes		24						24
plates	72	72						144
twiflers	120	120						240
muffins		24						24
bakers								
nappies	19	21						40
salts		12						12
table	211	273						484

	CC	EDG	DIPT	PAI	PRI	WILL	JAPAN	total
KITCHEN WARE								
bowls	24		57					81
jugs			8				6	14
mugs	12							12
kitchen	36		65				6	107
TOILET WARE								
hand basins	12							12
ewers	6							6
basins								
chambers	26							26
toilet	44							44

	CC	EDG	DIPT	PAI	PRI	WILL	JAPAN	total	%
tea				252				252	28.41
table	211	273						484	54.56
kitchen	36		65				6	107	12.06
toilet	44							44	4.96
	291	273	65	252			6	887	99.99

3 crates, numbered 28 through 30, Whitehaven Pottery, 1836

	CC	EDG	DIPT	PAI	PRI	WILL	JAPAN	total
TEA WARE								
teas unh				216				216
teas hnd								
Irish teas				24				24
bowls & saucers hnd				12				12
tea pots								
creams								
sugars								
tea				252				252
DINNER WARE								
dishes		24						24
plates		72						72
twiflers		120						120
muffins		24						24
bakers								
nappies	19	21						40
salts		18						18
dinner	19	279						298

	CC	EDG	DIPT	PAI	PRI	WILL	JAPAN	total
KITCHEN WARE								
bowls	36		138					174
jugs			16				6	22
mugs	36							36
kitchen	72		154				6	232
TOILET WARE								
ewers	6							6
hand basins	12							12
chambers	32							32
toilet	50							50

	CC	EDG	DIPT	PAI	PRI	WILL	JAPAN	total	%
tea				252				252	30.29
dinner	19	279						298	35.82
kitchen	72		154				6	232	27.88
toilet	50							50	6.01
	141	279	154	252			6	832	100.00

5 crates numbered 31 through 35, Whitehaven Pottery, 1836

	CC	EDG	DIPT	PAI	PRI	WILL	BLAK	CANE	total
TEA WARE									
teas hnd					144				144
tea pots					4		7	6	17
coffee pots					1				1
creams					4				4
cream ewers					4				4
sugars					2				2
tea muffins					36				36
tea					195		7	6	208
DINNER WARE									
dishes						8			8
plates		48				48			96
soups						24			24
twiflers		72							72
muffins						72			72
bakers						8			8
nappies								19	19
turtles		16							16
salts								12	12
cov. dishes						2			2
butters tubs					4				4
table		136			4	162		31	333

	CC	EDG	DIPT	PAI	PRI	WILL	BLAK	CANE	total
KITCHEN WARE									
bowls			84	12	27			81	204
jugs					18			22	40
mugs/cans								72	72
cake pans								10	10
kitchen			84	12	45			185	326
TOILET WARE									
ewers									
basins									
chambers	15				6			5	26
toilet	15				6			5	26

	CC	EDG	DIPT	PAI	PRI	WILL	BLAK	CANE	total	%
tea					195		7	6	208	23.29
table		136			4	162		31	333	37.29
kitchen			84	12	45			185	326	36.51
toilet	15				6			5	26	2.91
	15	136	84	12	250	162	7	227	893	100.0

5 crates numbered 36 through 40, Whitehaven Pottery, 1836

TEA WARE	CC	EDG	DIPT	PAI	PRI	WILL	total
teas unh							
teas hnd					288		288
tea pots					16		16
creams					8		8
cream ewers					4		4
sugars							
teas	---	---	---	---	316	---	316

DINNER WARE	CC	EDG	DIPT	PAI	PRI	WILL	total
dishes						16	16
plates	36	48				72	156
soups	12					24	36
twiflers	72	72					144
muffins						72	72
bakers						8	8
nappies	12						12
salts					6		6
peppers					6		6
mustards					6		6
table	132	120	---	---	18	192	462

KITCHEN WARE	CC	EDG	DIPT	PAI	PRI	WILL	total
bowls			84		33		117
jugs					39		39
kitchen	---	---	84	---	72	---	156

TOILET WARE	CC	EDG	DIPT	PAI	PRI	WILL	total
ewers	2				1		3
hand basins	6				1		7
chambers	15				1		16
toilet	23	---	---	---	3	---	26

	CC	EDG	DIPT	PAI	PRI	WILL	total	%
teas					316		316	32.92
table	132	120			18	192	462	48.12
kitchen			84		72		156	16.25
toilet	23				3		26	2.71
	---	---	---	---	---	---	---	
	155	120	84		409	192	960	100.00

The non-assorted crates from the Whitehaven Pottery, 1836

	CC	EDG	DIPT	PAI	CANE	PRINT	total
CRATE 7							
twiflers		1,020					1,020
CRATE 8							
twiflers	972						972
CRATE 9							
plates		444					444
soups		48					48
CRATE 10							
plates	462						462
soups	48						48
CRATE 11							
bowls	113		237	108			458
CRATE 12							
muffins	1,584	360					1,944
CRATE 13							
stand basins	160						160
CRATE 14							
mugs	138		132		114	72	456
jugs	42		48				90
cans						108	108

	CC	EDGED	DIPT	PAI	CANE	PRINT	total	%
PLATES	462	444					906	14.59
SOUPS	48	48					96	1.55
TWIFLERS	972	1,020					1,992	32.08
MUFFINS	1,584	360					1,944	31.30
BOWLS	113		237	108			458	7.38
JUGS	42		48				90	1.45
MUGS	138		132		114	72	456	7.34
CANS						108	108	1.74
STAND BASINS	160						160	2.58
	-----	-----	---	---	---	---	-----	-----
	3,519	1,872	417	108	114	180	6,210	100.01
	56.67	30.14	6.71	1.74	1.84	2.90		

CRATE SUMMARIES

TEAS	PAINTED	PRINTED	BROSLEY	total	%
London					
unhandled	3,996	864		4,860	56.02
handled		3,240		3,240	37.34
Irish					
unhandled					
handled	120	180	216	516	5.95
bowls & saucers					
unhandled					
handled	60			60	0.69
	-----	-----	----	-----	-----
	4,176	4,284	216	8,676	100.00
	48.13		51.87		

TEAS	PAINTED	PRINTED	BROSLEY	total	%
London					
unhandled	49.33	10.67		4,860	56.02
handled		40.00		3,240	37.34
Irish					
unhandled					
handled	120	180	216	516	5.95
bowls & saucers					
unhandled					
handled	60			60	0.69
	-----	-----	----	-----	-----
	4,176	4,284	216	8,676	100.00
	48.13		51.87		

TEA WARE	BLACK GLAZED	PAINTED	PRINTED	CANE	total	%
tea pots	35		203	30	268	33.13
coffee pots			5		5	0.62
creams		162	114		276	34.12
cream ewers			70		70	8.65
sugars			10		10	1.24
tea muffins			180		180	22.25
	---	---	----	---	----	-----
	35	162	582	30	809	100.01
	4.33	20.02	71.94	3.71		

DINNER WARE

	CC	EDGED	WILL	PRINT	LET	CANE	total	%
dishes		228	198	40			466	4.11
plates	624	1548	1008	240			3420	30.16
soups	60		240				300	2.65
twiflers	960	2352	348	240			3900	34.40
muffins		912	1128	240	972		3252	28.68
	----	-----	----	----	----	----	-----	-----
flat ware	1644	5040	2922	760	972		11338	100.00
percentages	14.50	44.45	25.77	6.70	8.57			

	CC	EDGED	WILL	PRINT	LET		total	%
dishes		48.93	42.49	8.58			466	4.11
plates	18.25	45.26	29.47	7.02			3420	30.16
soups	20.00		80.00				300	2.65
twiflers	24.62	60.31	8.92	6.15			3900	34.40
muffins		28.04	34.69	7.38	29.89		3252	28.68

	CC	EDGED	WILL	PRINT	LET	CANE	total	%
bakers			131	30			161	14.30
nappies	215	145				95	455	40.41
turtles		110					110	9.77
cov. dishes			10				10	0.89
butters tubs				30			30	2.66
salts		210	30			60	300	26.64
peppers			30				30	2.66
mustards			30				30	2.66
	---	-----	----	----	---	---	-----	------
hollow ware	215	465	231	60		155	1126	
percentages	19.09	41.30	20.50	5.33		13.77		

	CC	EDGED	WILL	PRINT	LET	CANE	total
grand total	1859	5505	3153	820	972	155	12464
flat ware	14.50	44.45	25.77	6.70	8.57		
hollow ware	19.09	41.30	20.50	5.33		13.77	
all table	14.91	44.17	25.30	6.58	7.80	1.24	

SUMMARIES, ASSORTED CRATES

KITCHEN WARE

	CC	DIPT	PRINT	JAP	PAINT	LET	CANE	total	%
bowls	450	2058	648		210		405	3771	62.43
jugs	102	64	487	30			110	793	13.13
mugs	462	316				288	360	1426	23.61
cake pans							50	50	0.83
kitchen	1041	2438	1135	30	210	288	925	6040	100.00
	16.79	40.36	18.79	0.5	3.48	4.77	15.31		

TOILET WARE

	CC	PRINTED	CANE	total	%
ewers	50	10		60	7.94
basins	166	10		176	23.28
chambers	455	40	25	520	68.78
	671	60	25	756	100.00
	88.76%	7.94%	3.31%		

According to a report in the *Whitehaven News* dated 1882, a new owner, a man called Brindle, invested a vast amount of money installing new plant and machinery. However he engaged Staffordshire craftsmen and it wasn't long before a strike ensued over pay differentials. Unfortunately the pottery was soon put up for sale again.

A new company was formed. The new partners were local men Mr T. Brown, Mr J.G. Dees and a Mr J.L. Paitson so the factory backstamp mark changed; it now became the Whitehaven Pottery Co., or W.P.Co. In a 1864 Directory of Whitehaven Messrs Dees and Paitson are recorded as Harbour Commissioners. According to the Whitehaven News of the 25th May, 1882 the price paid was £10,000 (this last record was researched by Mr Tom Scott, Mirehouse, Whitehaven). The Whitehaven Pottery closed in 1915.

From time to time I receive correspondence concerning people's potting forbears being connected in some way to our West Cumberland Potteries. Robert Pugh and Gareth Hughes in their book on the Llanelli Pottery, Wales, record the Guests leaving the Whitehaven Pottery and going to work at the Llanelli Pottery, Wales. David Guest, the second generation, became *Manager.* Also a man called Thomas Flower of Whitehaven, a potter, aged 41, is recorded in the 1851 census of Llanelli.

Lady Charlotte Schreiber married into the Guest family of Wales. One can imagine her listening to her husband's menfolk talking pots around the family dinner table each evening, enabling her to gain her vast expertise on the subject. Lady Charlotte had married the then great Ironmaster of Wales, his firm being known worldwide today, as Guest, Keen and Nettlefold. Her wonderful collection of British ceramics in the Victoria and Albert Museum is her memorial.

According to family correspondence, Richard Guest, son of George and Ann, born 1800, lived, and was baptised in Burslem, Staffordshire. However in 1820 Richard married Elizabeth Walker at St. James Church, Whitehaven. Elizabeth was the daughter of David and Sarah Walker of St. Bees, where Elizabeth was baptised in 1803. Richard is recorded as a *Glost Firer* at the Whitehaven Pottery, before going to the Llanelli Pottery, Wales.

Richard Guest, like James Brindley before him, left the Whitehaven Pottery when John Hall, a founder member, died in 1838, in Whitehaven. Census records for Burslem, 1841 show Richard and his wife living there at this time with their daughter Sarah, who had married Thomas Dewsbury, son of a Mariner, of Workington, Cumberland. Later that year (1841) Richard Guest had signed a contract with the South Wales Pottery, however he returned to Burslem a widower in 1851. His son David stayed on in Llanelli working in the office. For economic reasons the pottery closed down for a short while. When it reopened in 1870 David Guest was the Manager.

Sarah (nee Guest) and her husband Thomas Dewsbury (a pottery fireman) had a large family. Their eldest son Richard joined Uncle David to run the South Wales Pottery. David their second son became a ceramic artist. He trained at the Hill Pottery then went via Cauldon to join Royal Doulton, his speciality being Orchids. George, the third son, also trained to become a ceramic artist. He worked at Royal Doulton in the 1880s. His speciality was painting Fans. (*Family correspondence courtesy of Hilary Kydd, Kent.*).

Thomas Dewsbury husband of Sarah, née Guest was a pottery fireman, an important man at all potteries in the 19th century. It was his job to see that the saggers were placed in the position most suitable for their respective wares, as the temperature sustainable varies from pot to pot i.e. plates (pressed ware) will bear a higher temperature than cups (cast ware).

On a memorial headstone in Holy Trinity churchyard, Whitehaven, it records 'To the memory of Henry, son of Jeremiah and Jane Guest who departed this life at Falmouth, on the island of Jamaica, 24th July, 1812 aged 16 years'.

The following are lists of Whitehaven ships' cargoes of earthenware and their destinations, recorded in the *Whitehaven Gazette 1819-20*.

Date	Ships Name	Captain	Cargoes	Destination	Potter/Shipping Agent
10/05/1819	Mary		6 crates plus 6 hogsheads of earthenware plus 1 box of tobacco pipes	St. Johns New Brunswick, Canada	Thomas and Joseph Brocklebank Shipping Agents
24/05/1819	William	George McQuaid	1,800 pieces of blackware	Belfast, Northern Ireland	Joseph Richardson, The Ginns House pottery, Whitehaven

Date	Ships Name	Captain	Cargoes	Destination	Potter/Shipping Agent
11/06/1819	Lion	Wm. Farish	22 crates of earthenware 1,000 pieces 900 pieces	Belfast Northern Ireland	Woodnorth, Harrison and Hall, The Whitehaven pottery. Jas. Goulding the Glass House pottery Whitehaven Jas. Richardson the Ginns House pottery Whitehaven.
11/06/1819	Anne		40 crates of earthenware	Terceira the Azores, Portuguese Territory.	Thomas Burrell Shipping Agent.
11/06/1819	William		9 boxes of tobacco pipes plus 360 pieces of earthenware	Donagdee N. Ireland	Woodnorth, Harrison and Hall, the Whitehaven pottery.
11/06/1819	Lion	Wm. Farish	2 crates of earthenware plus 9 crates of earthenware	Belfast Northern Ireland	Woodnorth, Harrison and Hall the Whitehaven pottery.
11/06/1819	Isabella Jane		1 crate of earthenware	Strangford Northern Ireland	Woodnorth, Harrison and Hall, the Whitehaven pottery.
11/06/1819	Prince		3 crates of earthenware	Ramsey, Isle of Man	Jas. Goulding the Glass House pottery Whitehaven.
14/06/1819	Lion		3 crates of tobacco pipes plus 2 crates of tobacco pipes plus 9 crates of earthenware	Belfast Northern Ireland	Woodnorth, Harrison and Hall the Whitehaven pottery.

Date	Ships Name	Captain	Cargoes	Destination	Potter/Shipping Agent
21/06/1819	Farmer	James	10 crates of earthenware plus 2,140 loose pieces plus 2 boxes of tobacco pipes	Belfast Northern Ireland	The Master
21/06/1819	Ally and Nancy	Edward Mylcrea	1 crate of earthenware	Douglas Isle of Man	Jas. Goulding the Glass House pottery Whitehaven
21/06/1819	Trafalger	Robert Carron	1 crate of earthenware	Derby haven Isle of Man	Jas. Goulding the Glass House pottery
25/06/1819	Lion	Wm. Farish	11 crates of earthenware	Belfast Northern Ireland	Woodnorth, Harrison and Hall, the Whitehaven Pottery.
25/06/1819	Grampus	Wm. Lewin	2 crates of earthenware 1 crate of earthenware	Douglas Isle of Man	James Allinson Retailer. T. Pearson Retailer.
28/06/1819	Elizabeth	Hugh Ferguson	1 crate of earthenware plus 1 box of tob. pipes	Belfast Northern Ireland	The Master
26/06/1819	Catherine	Wm. Tear	5 crates of earthenware	Peel, Isle of Man	The Master
05/07/1819	Farmer	Jas. Gibbons	2,140 pieces of earthenware plus 2 boxes of Tobacco pipes.	Strangford Northern Ireland	The Master
26/07/1819	New Triton	Hugh Beedon	2 crates of earthenware plus 1 box of Tobacco pipes	Douglas Isle of Man	Jas. Goulding the Glass House pottery, Whitehaven
30/07/1819	Jane McCleary	M. Tomalty	1 crate of earthenware plus 6 crates earthenware	Strangford Northern Ireland.	The Master Woodnorth, Harrison and Hall, the Whitehaven pottery.

Date	Ships Name	Captain	Cargoes	Destination	Potter/Shipping Agent
06/08/1819	Shamrock	John Clark	1 box Tobacco pipes plus 3 crates of earthenware	Strangford Northern Ireland.	Woodnorth, Harrison and Hall, the Whitehaven pottery.
06/08/1819	Fancy		252 pieces of earthenware plus 1 box of Tobacco pipes.	Douglas Isle of Man	The Master
06/08/1819	The Delight		1 crate of earthenware	Kirkcudbright-shire, Scotland	Isobel Clarke, Retailer
13/08/1819	Henry Harding	J. Wheeler	18 crates of earthenware	Strangford Northern Ireland	Woodnorth, Harrison and Hall, the Whn. pottery
13/08/1819	John and Mary Ann	J. Wilkinson	600 pieces of earthenware	Ramsey Isle of Man	Jas. Goulding the Glass House pottery Whitehaven.
13/08/1819	Mary		1 crate of earthenware plus 1 hamper	Derby haven Isle of Man.	Jas. Goulding the Glass House pottery Whitehaven
13/08/1819	The Lion	Wm. Farish	22 crates of earthenware plus 570 pieces	Belfast Northern Ireland	Woodnorth, Harrison and Hall the Whitehaven pottery.
05/11/1819	The Mayflower	J. Potts	7 crates of earthenware	Antigua	H. and R. Jefferson Agents
05/11/1819	The Eleanor	J. Stowell	4 crates of earthenware plus 1 trunk plus 2 boxes of Tobacco pipes.	Strangford Northern Ireland	Woodnorth, Harrison and Hall the Whitehaven pottery.
12/11/1819	The Diligent	From Harrington Harbour	4 crates of Delft (See Eliz. Adams NCS re Isle of Man advertisement dated 1814).	Dublin, Eire.	Woodnorth, Harrison and Hall the Whitehaven pottery

Date	Ships Name	Captain	Cargoes	Destination	Potter/Shipping Agent
20/11/1819	Esther and John		4 crates of earthenware	Belfast Northern Ireland	Woodnorth, Harrison and Hall, the Whitehaven Pottery
07/01/1820	Jane McClear		45 crates of earthenware	Londonderry, Northern Ireland	Woodnorth, Harrison and Hall, Whn. pottery
17/02/1820	Albion	Dobson	9 crates of earthenware	Antigua	Woodnorth, Harrison and Hall the Whitehaven pottery
04/02/1820	Brown		18 crates of earthenware	Belfast Northern Ireland	Woodnorth, Harrison and Hall, Whn. pottery
28/02/1820	Thetis		20 crates of earthenware	Antigua	R. Barker and Sons, Agents
13/03/1820	Farmer	Tear	9 crates plus 700 pieces of earthenware	Strangford	Woodnorth, Harrison and Hall, Whn. pottery Jos. Richardson the Ginns House. Pottery Whn.
13/03/1820	Commerce	Appleby	6 boxes of Tobacco pipes plus one crate of earthenware	Belfast Northern Ireland	Woodnorth, Harrison and Hall, the Whitehaven pottery
27/03/1820	New Triton	Hugh Beadon	1 crate of earthenware	Douglas Isle of Man	Master
27/03/1820	William and Mary	Kennedy	3 crates of earthenware	Douglas Isle of Man	Master
03/04/1820	Sophia	Colman	8 crates of earthenware.	Dublin (Eire)	Jos.Richardson The Ginns House Pottery, Whitehaven.
17/04/1820	Traveller	Carr	1 box of earthenware.	Jamaica	Master

Date	Ships Name	Captain	Cargoes	Destination	Potter/Shipping Agent
17/04/1820	North Star	W. Ostle	2 crates of earthenware	Chatham then known as Buctush Canada (Changed in 1843.)	Master
17/04/1820	Elizabeth Ann	Crooks	1 hogshead of earthenware	Miramichi and New Brunswick	Jas. Goulding the Glass House Pottery, Whn.
01/05/1820	Eleanor	Stowell	11 crates of earthenware plus 1 hogshead plus 3 tierces plus 5 boxes of Tobacco pipes	Strangford Northern Ireland	Woodnorth, Harrison and Hall, the Whitehaven pottery.
11/06/1820	New Triton	Ruddick	1 crate of earthenware	Douglas Isle of Man	Jas. Goulding the Glass House pottery Whn.
07/11/1820	London	Vardy	1 crate of earthenware.	Ramsey Isle of Man	R. Curwen, Agent
07/11/1820	Canda	Potts	2 crates of earthenware.	Richibucto, South America	Woodnorth, Harrison and Hall, the Whitehaven pottery.
07/11/1820	St. Patrick	Killip	1 crate of earthenware plus 1 tierce	Douglas Isle of Man	Woodnorth, Harrison and Hall, the Whitehaven pottery.
24/11/1820	Isabella Jane	Crail	300 pieces of earthenware	Strangford	Master

Courtesy of Mr R. Pearson, St Bees for sight of *The Whitehaven Gazette*.

References
A Hogshead is a barrel which usually holds 56 gallons.
A Tierce is a medium barrel usually for wine.
These would be brought back to Whitehaven full of Rum etc.

It is recorded rags were being imported into Whitehaven to make rough paper for packaging pottery for export.

The Lowther Cash Books dated 1785, 86, 87 & 88.
4th October 1803

Ships importing for the Whitehaven Potteries

Date	Ships Name	Captain	Cargoes	From	Potter/Shipping Agent
10/05/1819	Liver	Unknown	64 tons of pipe clay	Poole, Dorset	Whitehaven pottery
17/05/1819	Robert	Unknown	10,000 basket rods	Kirkcudbright-shire	Whitehaven pottery
21/05/1819	James	Unknown	50 tons of pipe clay	Poole, Dorset	Whitehaven pottery
21/05/1819	The Supply	Robert Carron	1 barrel of glass	Liverpool	Woodnorth Harrison and Hall, Whitehaven pottery
24/05/1819	Mercury	Jas. Barton	2 tons of pipe clay	Liverpool	Jas.Allison 31/05/1819
31/05/1819	The Brittania	Jas. Broadford	2 tons of tobacco pipe clay	Liverpool	Woodnorth, Harrison and Hall, Whitehaven pottery
04/06/1819	Brittania	Unknown	50 tons of pipe clay	Poole, Dorset	Whitehaven pottery
30/07/1819	Bettes	Unknown	50 tons of pipe clay, 23 casks of ground flint	Thomas Jones, Beaumaris	Whitehaven pottery
18/10/1819	Nimble	Unknown	3 hhds clay 3 tierces of clay	Liverpool	Whitehaven pottery
10/01/1819	Bettes	Unknown	50 tons of pipe clay	Beaumaris	Whitehaven pottery
24/04/1819	Despatch	Unknown	120 tons of pipe clay	Teignmouth	Whitehaven pottery
08/05/1820	Bettes	Unknown	50 tons of pipe clay. 11 casks of ground flint	Beaumaris	Whitehaven pottery

Annie Englesham Thesis Ph.D. Part 1977 – Lancaster University, Carlisle CRO

West Cumberland Shipping 1680-1800 – Whitehaven Port Books – Cargoes:-

Page 112

We imported from Liverpool earthenware - 15 crates, each crate to contain:-

5 milk pans	3s. 4d.
24 diptware	2s. 2d.
12 cups	6d.
1 yellow dish	4d.
2 cyder jugs	2d.

TEAWARES

The people of Holland were the first Europeans to drink tea or cha as it was called by the Chinese. The Dutch people poured their tea into their tea bowls to cool and drunk from the saucer. In the 19th century many paintings feature tea being drunk with different mannerisms regarding the handling of tea bowls, especially by the ladies. Some held their bowls between thumb and forefinger, whilst others held their smallest finger as if reaching for the sky.

The East India Co. wished to supply the Americans with tea direct, at 10/-s. instead of via Great Britain and costing 20/-s., hence the *Boston tea party* of 1773, when colonists dumped three shiploads of tea directly into Boston harbour which is the reason this poem, featured in the Cumberland Pacquet newspaper 20/10/1774 was written.

Farewell the Tea board with its Equipage
Of Cups and Saucers, Cream Buckets, Sugar Tongs
The Pretty Tea Chest also lately stored
With Ceylon, Congo and best Double Fine
Full many a joyous moment have I sat by ye
Hearing the Girls Tale, the Old Maids talk Scandal
And the Spruce Coxcomb laugh – at may be nothing
No more shall I dish out the once loved liquor
Though now detestable
Because I'm taught (and believe it true)
Its use will fasten slavish chains upon my country
To reign triumphant in America.

Early in the 19th century, the tax on tea was abolished and imports of tea from the far east jumped by some 400%. It usually cost 10/-s to 16/-s per lb so was kept under lock and key by the master of the household, in wooden tea caddies which showed one compartment for green and one for black tea. These tea casks were usually wood veneered; the leaf tea went into an inner lead container. Nowadays they fetch good prices at auction.

This Whitehaven Pottery 'Erin' pattern teacup and saucer is in the Alton Museum in Hampshire, part of the Michael Bertoud Collection illustrated in his book *A Compendium of British Cups*. It is the only example recorded to date. See page 63, for a photograph of factory wasters in blue/white and brown/white.

Saucer in the Erin pattern see shards on page 63.
(Courtesy of Joyce Chitty, Hest Bank)

The Temperance Movement began in Northamptonshire; it soon became widely supported and encouraged at this time, by many factory and colliery owners, in order to keep their men away from the evil of alcohol. They provided tea houses which were a meeting place, as well as afternoon tea dances, which were social occasions and an acceptable pastime.

Mid 19th century John Wilkinson gave a thanks-giving-tea in the Temperance Hall in Whitehaven to his workforce, in appreciation of their valiant efforts in saving his pottery during a large fire at the adjacent Copperas Works.

Recently a local couple showed me their family heirloom. It was a small white creamer and sugar basin, in soft paste porcelain with blue sprigging. I went along to see the Collections Officer at that time in the Beacon in Whitehaven, *Craig Hutchinson*. We opened box after box, finally I gleefully exclaimed, we have a matching mould. I also had many shards.

The small creamer and sugar bowl, sprigged, is soft paste porcelain, this mould is in the Beacon Collection, Whitehaven.

Ironically, shortly after this Mrs Peggy Stubbs, then Vice President of Bootle W.I. in South Cumbria, brought me what she thought was an earthenware rumbutter bowl in the Brosely pattern (a family heirloom).

Broseley pattern large slop bowl owned by Mrs Peggy Stubbs.

Broseley pattern a small sprigged creamer sucrier gifted to the author in 2004 by Peggy Stubbs, Bootle W.I. (It was a collection of 100 pieces) Kindly restored for me by Dr John Black, (Lecturer on Delft).

It had been bought off the travelling salesmen from the Whitehaven pottery by her husband's grandmother. These salesmen were trusted by the local community. One would take a watch into town to be repaired, or a pair of clogs to be bottomed, these would be returned on the next visit. For this small favour he would be invited to share a meal with the farming families. He also brought news of local births, deaths and marriages but would never gossip, that would have caused friction. Local sporting news whether it be pigeons, football, rugby or horse racing was always welcome.

Peggy's rum butter bowl was a slop bowl, part of a large farmhouse tea service, (in the Irish Size) the same as those quoted in the customs documents for 1836 under the title Earthenware despatched to America. See page 49. The Broseley pattern is also recorded in the list of patterns. Peggy went away smiling, telling me her slop bowl would always be the family rumbutter bowl!

I told her I could imagine her husband's forebears sitting around their large farmhouse table with this tea service consisting of a large teapot, 12 large teacups and saucers, the sucrier (full of sugar lumps), an extra large milk jug (say two pints), a cake tazza and plates, which would be full of lovely home baked bread, ginger bread, teacakes and fruit cakes. A substantial Sunday afternoon treat for all hard working farming folks.

Finally, having proof of the manufacture of softpaste porcelain, I started to study the many photographs of local family heirlooms I had recorded during the past two decades, mainly a hand-painted part tea service and lovely jugs, a couple of which are in the Beacon Collection, Whitehaven.

I have no doubt the seascape scenes on an Irish Size part tea service, were painted by members of our famous Whitehaven Marine School of Painters. Some may even have tried their hand at flower painting on the jugs; the gilding around the neck frills is expertly done. We certainly had workmen capable of doing such work at this time.

The painting on the factory marked Hillis Bowl is proof of this. It is from the W.H.H. era i.e. 1812-1819. The Whitehaven Marine School of Painters went to Liverpool mid nineteenth century. Courtesy of *Miss Anne Dick, Local Studies Librarian, Whitehaven recently retired.*

Bohemia pattern, on cup and saucer shards in blue white. Approximate date 1820. See mark and initials.

Cyrene pattern on cups and saucers in blue/white and brown/white, plus the mark. We have recorded no whole pots in this pattern to date. 1820 period.

At the N.C.S. 2007 Summer School at Chester I was shown a blue and white plate depicting the 'Bohemia' pattern like the shards on the previous page, and marked. Courtesy of the owner I was given permission to photograph it and include it in this book.

The plate and the mark 'Bohemia' and initials I.W. John Wilkinson, Whitehaven pottery 1820.

Erin pattern in blue/white and brown/white. Only one cup/saucer is recorded in this pattern, (Erin is the old name for Ireland). See Michael Berthoud in his book a Compendium of British Cups, page 173.

These are saucer shards. Top right is a biscuit shard, in a pattern I call Harebell. It is the inside pattern on the Nanking jugs, which depict a chinoiserie design on the outside. See page 66.

Shards of the pattern Sea Leaf in a variety of colours, blue/white, green/white and black/white plus biscuit shards.

Marseillaise pattern shards in a variety of colours, flow/blue, brown/white and green/white plus an impressed mark.

Some interesting handle shards. The centre shard is the handle off a tooth brush holder, see Toilet wares. Also note the '9' shaped cup handles.

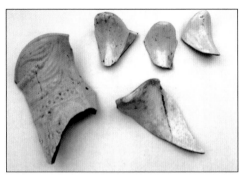

'Jug spouts', the one on the left shows a mould of a sheaf of corn. The one on the right is the Admiral Duncan Ale Jug spout.

A Milk Jug. In a private collection.

Bishops Court House, Ballough, *the Beacon Collection,Whitehaven.*

The emblem of the Isle of Man is depicted on the front of this small milk jug (made approx. 1820-40). A Paddle Steamer is depicted on the reverse of the jug. The Isle of Man Steam Navigation Company had an office here in Whitehaven and various steamers took passengers across to the island. Note the spurs on the heel of the boots like those on the excavated shard. The border can be seen on the *Free Trade* printed items and the *Isaac Sloan Money Boxes.* The black printed teapot depicts a large house on the island.

Excavated shards, the large shard depicts Peel Castle according to Shirley and Roger Edmundson, frequent summer visitors to the island. One can see the spurs, as depicted on the emblem of the I.o.M.

Small creamer, sprigged, owners are local people. A second, (dirt in glaze).

St. Bees Church and College. A Theological College which opened approx., 1816. A bat print. (Courtesy of Wendy Mitton, Carlisle).

Basalt sucrier, mould in the Beacon. Collection of moulds.

Blackware teapot, (private collection).

Bone china cup and saucers inscribed The Church and Cottage, St. Bees (please note the new tower). These are in private collections.

A small underglaze brown/white printed coffee cup and saucer, the centre shows a girl with a large sheep, they are surrounded by a border of flora and fauna prints, the mark is extremely rare; it shows a small hut under a palm tree and I.W., the initials of John Wilkinson the owner, so a 1820-24 pot. Pet Lamb, name discovered in April, 2008.

Fabric pattern, underglaze printed on a one pint mug, Peggy Stubbs, Bootle.

The Free trade print on a frog mug and loving cup, the Beacon Collection, Whitehaven.

A lustreware sucrier, owner, a Wigton lady, part of a tea service.

Two Nanking patterned jugs. Owner Mrs Wendy Mitton, Carlisle.

A Large Pekin patterned jug. Author's collection.

Both these Nanking and Pekin jugs were included in the Wedgwood Museum, True Blue Exhibition, held at Barleston, Staffordshire, in 1998.

A one pint mug which shows the Keeping School print.

Cockermouth Castle Cup and handle.

A large mug Terrace pattern (in a private collection). The author owns an identical mug printed in underglaze brown/white. These are rare items. This one is marked I.W.

The Romp print on small mug and a Whitehaven Darning Egg. The Mug border print is on the Whitehaven Pottery Money boxes and loving cups.

A pair of Felspathic sprigged jugs in the Beacon Collection, Whitehaven, together with the neck mould, these are very translucent.

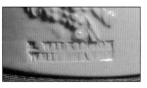

A large coffee pot, the centre photograph shows the rare impressed mark R. Wilkinson, Whitehaven.

A moulded one pint mug, treacle glazed. It depicts Youth and Old Age.

Blue jug, gilded and dated to Capt. Glover of the Brig. Massereene. Built in Belfast, 1813. Owned by Joseph Mullen and others. In the Beacon Collection, Whitehaven. (See Cumberland Shipping, by Sawyers, republished by M. Moon, Whitehaven).

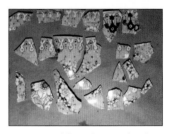

This unique cup and saucer is in the Amoy pattern, plus excavated shards, marked I.W.

A Moss Rose pattern milk jug plus wasters in blue/white underglaze printed. Shards on the right show the distinctive inside rim. In the Chapter headed Miscellaneous there is a baby's feeding bottle in this pattern which was also made by Mintons.

The common Rhine pattern, on a morning size cup and saucer Author's Collection.

Rhine on a Mug in Muncaster Castle.

Blue Sprigging on a trio of jugs, prunus blossom, suggests the new Japanese influence on art approx. 1890. The Beacon Collection, Whitehaven.

The Whitehaven pottery marriage puzzle jug depicting before and after marriage (smiling and grimacing at each other). The mark W.P.Co. Whitehaven, (Whitehaven Pottery Company) therefore made after 1882.   *Owners of the jug Mr and Mrs Coffee, Whitehaven.*

The Glass House School Coronation Mug depicting H.M. Queen Victoria, June, 1838. Photo taken 1980s, with kind permission of the late owner Mrs Charles Humphreys Senior. This mug was sold recently and fetched £850 plus. However there are others in the Beacon Collection, Whitehaven.

Many years ago, a local lady showed me her part tea service, depicting hand painted sea and landscapes with gilding. It was in soft paste porcelain (a white body). When I have visited local people in the past, they have often shown me their family heirlooms, jugs, etc., in a soft paste porcelain, in the same very white body, hand painted with tulips or roses, initialled and gilded. Unfortunately I let them down gently and explained how *then* I had no proof that the Whitehaven pottery had produced soft paste porcelain, now I hear we did.

The bowl on the left is a slop bowl, on the right a cup and saucer both are depicting landscapes, the body is soft paste porcelain. These are remnants of a morning size tea service. They are finely gilded and beautifully hand painted.

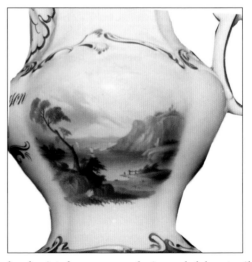

The inscribed Joseph Benn Dawson jug with a hand painted seascape on the jug and elaborate gilding. A family heirloom, (local) dated 1848.

A pair of jugs, finely decorated and gilded, in The Beacon Collection, Whitehaven.

An enamelled christening mug which depicts the bloody hand of Ulster. It is inscribed to James Perkins, and is dated 1848. It is owned by a local family.This hand is on the flag of Ulster. Many local men were shipped out from Whitehaven to fight in the troubles in Ireland in the 19th century.

There is no doubt in my mind that during the period 1824-1848, the quality of the hand decorated pots which I have recorded, prove the Whitehaven pottery had engaged or had persuaded a member of the local Marine School of Painters to paint for the pottery. This would have been an extra source of income for them.

A cup chock or former excavated on the site.

71

Teawares with blue sponging on the edges.

Dipped ware, cup shards top in a blue ceramic paint.

A tea service depicting a local church. Note metal swing lid on the tall hot water jug and the rare sliding lid on the teapot, plus a moustache cup. Underglaze printed in black. A family heirloom (local).

An 1851 Exhibition item, the extra large Rum butter bowl, printed in pink. Presented by Miss Edith Sandwith to Whitehaven Museum.

Willow pattern shards.

Blue Sponged Teaware.

The early Whitehaven Pottery teawares depict chinoiserie designs, i.e. Willow, Nanking, Amoy, Bohemia (strange, as this is the name for part of the Czech Republic) Brosely and Mandarin with long pipe.

In the early nineteenth century the introduction of colours on earthenware involved the potters starting to use chrome, green and pink. Artists and poets had started to travel to Europe, the scenes they captured were soon incorporated on factory pots. At Whitehaven we have Bosphorus, Rhine, Marseillaise and Pekin, (whilst the name suggests it is oriental, the pattern shows a European scene).

The Whitehaven Pottery's American customers favoured mulberry, brown and flow blue colours, as well as fauna and flora patterns on the pots we despatched to them.

The Violin Pattern

Whilst attending a ceramic seminar organised by Wendy Mitton at Carlisle in 2002, I placed some shards on a table. Immediately, the very experienced ceramist, Mr Roger Edmundson picked up my cup shard shown right, and exclaimed the 'Violin' pattern. I'm afraid, I knew nothing of this pattern at the time however whilst researching the Tea Party print, amongst the colour plates in The True Blue Exhibition Catalogue on 'rare blue printed earthenware', placed next to a Tea Party printed teapot, a second teapot

A cup shard in underglaze blue/white, the Violin pattern.

is illustrated and recorded as being printed with the Violin pattern, *Maker Unknown*, approx., 1800-1815, Ref. Case 34/15". I wonder.

Taken from *The Catalogue of the True Blue Exhibition* held at the Wedgwood Museum, Barleston, Stoke on Trent, 21st March to 12th July, 1998. To celebrate the 25th Anniversary of The Friends of Blue, with kind permission of the Wedgwood Trustees, courtesy of the Curator Miss Gaye Blake Roberts.

On the left a teapot depicting the Tea Party print, on the right the Violin print, recorded Maker Unknown.

TEAWARES OF THE WEST CUMBERLAND POTTERIES

OBJECT	PATTERN NAME	WHOLE POT/SHARD	ORIGIN	DESCRIPTION	MARK/DATE
1. Small sucrier and cream jug	Blue sprigged	Whole pots	Local man	A soft paste body with blue sprigging, moulds are in the Beacon Colleetion Whitehaven	1840-63
2. Butter tubs these would hold half pound.	Creamware, yellow in colour.	A butter bowl was excavated intact, also shards of butter tubs in the 1994 site dig.	Douglas Burn site in the centre of Whitehaven.	Finely potted objects. See documents dated 1772 from America.	1772 see documents From Professor George Miller and Asst. Prof. Dr Anne-Smart Martin, U.S.A.
3. Morning cup (Irish size) large.	MARSEILLAISE	One whole cup, plenty of shards. A common Whitehaven pottery pattern	Purchased from a Whitehaven dealer	Earthenware, thickly potted, a good glaze. Reported in N.C.S. Qtrly Newsletter No. 111 September, 1998 page 23, figure 9.	1820-40 no mark.
4. Morning cup and saucer (Irish size) large.	AMOY	Whole cup and saucer plus shards of this pattern.	Local lady who allowed me to photograph her pots in 1984.	These two pieces are unique, up to press. Shards reported in N.C.S. Quarterly Newsletter No. 111 Sept., '98 page 10, figure 6.	I.W. 1820-24 mark on reverse.
5. Morning cup and saucer. (Irish size) large	RHINE	Whole cup and saucer.	This cup and saucer was given to the Author by two friends fellow ceramicists in 1990. Excavated biscuit shards depicted the pips.	Earthenware, underglaze printed, in blue/white. Cup has a gold line around the rim. The pips on the handle are identical to those on three other recorded items of Whitehaven pottery i.e. a cereal bowl, a puzzle jug and a toilet bowl (or baking bowl) in the willow pattern.	This pattern was made by most potteries. 1820-73.

TEAWARES OF THE WEST CUMBERLAND POTTERIES – *Continued*

OBJECT	PATTERN NAME	WHOLE POT/SHARD	ORIGIN	DESCRIPTION	MARK/DATE
6. Shards only of Teawares, glazed and unglazed.	Top section has been dipped in a blue colouring and the bottom section glazed with a white slip.	Shards only, and plentiful. Like today's Cornish ware, it must have been a popular pattern.	Whitehaven pottery site.	Earthenware. Reported in the quarterly N.C.S. Newsletter No. 111, Sept., 1998, page, 16 figure 6.	1860 approx. no marks
7. Two saucers	Mandarin with Long Pipe. Named by Helen Hallesy author of the Glamorgan Potteries Book.	Two saucers plus many shards printed in pale blue/ white, brown/white and a darker shade of blue/white.	Whitehaven pottery site	Reported in the N.C.S. Qtrly Newsletter No. 111, Sept., 1998 page 25, figure 16. brown/ white and blue/ white under the glaze printed. Both saucers depict the Mandarin smoking his long pipe. He is joined by his family who are leaning against a chair.	The Whitehaven saucer is marked with an impressed star which appears on many of the Whitehaven pots.
8. Tea cups, plates and Saucer.	BOHEMIA	Shards plus plates recently discovered Aug, 2007	Whitehaven pottery site, excavated in in 1994.	Mandarin sitting under a belltoy (umbrella) smoking his pipe and admiring his garniture of 3 vases. Underglaze printed in pale blue and white. reported in the N.C.S. Qtrly Newsletter No. 111 Sept, 1998 Page 23, fig. 11.	1820-40 I.W. marked and named on many shards.
9. 4 Large Milk Jugs	NANKING	Whole pots and shards.	Whitehaven pottery site, shards reported.	Shards depict the inside border of harebells. The main scene is Chinoiserie.	I.W. marked 1820-24.

75

TEAWARES OF THE WEST CUMBERLAND POTTERIES – *Continued*

OBJECT	PATTERN NAME	WHOLE POT/SHARD	ORIGIN	DESCRIPTION	MARK/DATE
10. Shards of cups and saucers.	ERIN the old name for Ireland.	Shards only underglaze printed in brown/white	A cup which is unique and is illustrated in Michael Berthoud's cup book, page 173, plate 1037.	The book a 'Compendium of British Cups' describes the shards thus 'Musical Pastimes in a cartouche' which surrounds the border of the saucer. Reported in the N.C.S. Qtrly newsletter No. 111, Sept. 1998 page 20 figure 1.	Our shards show the pattern name of ERIN.
11. Two blue/white Jugs one large and one small.	PEKIN	The two whole pots in this pattern are marked.	These two jugs were purchased by my husband at Messrs Mitchells Auction Co., Cockermouth, one in 1995 and one in 2001.	Underglaze printed in blue/ white, well potted. The larger of the two jugs was displayed in the True Blue Exhibition at Barleston, Staffs. They depict oriental type boats with mountains. The background depicts a European type of castle.	I.W. Mark on the reverse 1820-40.
12. Cups and saucers.	Cups blue sponged, saucer centre has been left in the white.	Shards only.	Whitehaven pottery site.	No pots to date. Everyday ware. A child's plate shows the same sponging technique.	1820-40 no mark.
13. Cups and saucers.	GOTHIC	Shards only.	Whitehaven pottery site dig.	Underglaze printed in brown/white reported in N.C.S. Quarterly Newsletter No. 111 Page 22, fig. 8.no mark	1820-40 no mark

TEAWARES OF THE WEST CUMBERLAND POTTERIES – *Continued*

OBJECT	PATTERN NAME	WHOLE POT/SHARD	ORIGIN	DESCRIPTION	MARK/DATE
14. Coffee Cup and saucer	SEALEAF	Shards underglaze printed in blue/white. A coffee cup and saucer, (miniature) is underglaze printed in black/white. Also a fire damaged shard shows this print.	Whitehaven pottery site reported in the N.C.S. Quarterly Newsletter No. 111 Sept., '98 page 1 fig. 7.	Underglaze printed nice back stamp shows part words --- LEAF and another SEA--- The name is surrounded by fibre.	Marked 1820-72
15. Milk jug and small plate. Sucrier Slop Bowl and Egg cup	BROSELY	Whole pots and shards some of these are owned by President of Bootle W.I. Peggy Stubbs	Volume 1, The History of the West Cumb. Potteries Page 41, figs 1,2,3 and 4.	Pale blue/white printed, sometimes an impressed star mark. Teasets were shipped to the USA in 1836, see lists.	1836 data on USA invoice naming pattern on pots and quantity.
16. Chocolate cups.	MAYFIELD	Shards only to date.	Whitehaven pottery site.	See NCS Newsletter 111, Sept., 98, page 22, fig.5 underglaze blue/white printed.	Many shards showing the name.
17. Tea cups and saucers.	CYRENE	Shards only to date.	Whitehaven pottery site.	Earthenware, underglaze printed in brown/white and blue/white.	Name and the initials I.W. 1820, also the mark of a small 'eye' which is painted on under the glaze.
18. Coffee cup and saucer.	PET LAMB PRINT	Restored handle.	Bought off a dealer in Whitehaven by my husband in 1985.	Underglaze printed in brown/white, earthenware. The centre of the saucer a girl is feeding a large sheep/ or goat There is also a large house in the background.	Initialled I.W. underneath a Palm tree which hangs over a small hut? 1820 A rare mark.

TEAWARES OF THE WEST CUMBERLAND POTTERIES – *Continued*

OBJECT	PATTERN NAME	WHOLE POT/SHARD	ORIGIN	DESCRIPTION	MARK/DATE
19. Lustreware teaset.	PINK LUSTRE as advertised in the 'Isle of Man Gazette', 1814.	Whole pots plus shards.	A lady in Wigton	Sucrier lid is identical in shape to those on the Whitehaven pottery tobacco jars.	1814 - date of Isle of Man advertisement Inserted in the Gazette Newspaper.
20. Tea cup.	VIOLIN	Shards only	Whitehaven pottery site.	Earthenware, underglaze printed in blue/white see N.C.S. Qrtly Newsletter No. 111 Sept., 1998 Page 24, figure 8.	No mark 1824-72.
21. Five locally inscribed teapots in creamware.	Inscribed, under the glaze.	Whole pots. 'Weary Hall' is the seat of Mr Charles Drewry, also 'Camerton and Seaton, 630-1900' by Herbert and Mary Jackson who refer to Christopher Curwen and Ann Porter of 'Weary Hall' who succeeded to the 'Camerton Estate, 12th Nov. 1708. This was where Aaron Wedgwood I of West Cumberland and Margaret nee (Tunstall) started off their married life.	Made at the Whitehaven pottery, in today's Market Place, or at the Scilly Banks or at St. Bees by Aaron Wedgwood III of West Cumberland.	See N.C.S. Newsletter No. 96 page 40 also No.115 September, 1999, page 30.	1. Inscribed Molly Drewry Weary Hall 1773. 2. Inscribed Sussana Drewry, Weary Hall, 1768. 3. Inscribed Ester Saul, Beckfoot and shows the initials M.D. it is impressed WEDGWOOD under the base. 4. Inscribed Mary Saul Beckfoot. 5. Inscribed Sam Abbot and Margrett Bowman, Whitehaven ,1770

TEAWARES OF THE WEST CUMBERLAND POTTERIES – *Continued*

OBJECT	PATTERN NAME	WHOLE POT/SHARD	ORIGIN	DESCRIPTION	MARK/DATE
22. Creamware Milk Jug	Bat printed in black, inscribed.	Whole pot	A present to author.	Shows discolouration but a nice print, inscribed Church and College.	1820
23. Handleless teabowls in creamware.	No decoration	Whole pots and shards	Douglas Burn site in today's Whitehaven Market Place.	Very fragile, saltglazed and excavated on site, helped by girl pupils from nearby St. Bees school.	1772 see Shipping Invoice. For 1772.
24. Saucer	Print of St. Bees Church.	Whole pot	Local farmer's wife in St. Bees village.	Bone china, the words differ from creamware milk jug 'Church and School' see No. 22.	1820-40
25. A whole tea set, plus candle stick and snuffer.	Print of the local West Cumberland Church of Arlecdon.	A local man.	Family heirloom.	Water Jug has a metal lid. Bone china.	1840-72.
26. Coffee can	Church and School of St. Bees	Whole pot	A local person.	The print is identical to No. 24 and is bone china.	1820-40.
27. Milk Jug	Print of an I.o.M. 'Paddle Steamer' emblem on the reverse.	Whole pot and shards.	A local person.	A large shard depicts Peel Castle, Isle of Man.	19th century.
28. Pint Mugs	1. Free Trade 2. The Terrace	Whole pots.	1. Beacon Collection. 2. Local Man also author.	1. Underglaze printed in black/white showing the popular Whitehaven pottery border. 2. Print of a couple walking along the terrace of a large house plus a peacock.	19th century.

TEAWARES OF THE WEST CUMBERLAND POTTERIES – Continued

OBJECT	PATTERN NAME	WHOLE POT/SHARD	ORIGIN	DESCRIPTION	MARK/DATE
28. Pint Mugs *Continued*	3. The Romp on reverse Keeping School / 4. Treacle glazed with moulding depicting boy putties pulling a large goat. / 5. Fabric Pattern	Whole pots.	3. Author. / 4. Local lady / 5. Local Person.	3. Print of a girl skipping, this is also on the darning eggs / 4. Treacleglazed over a yellow clay body. / 5. Even the handle of this mug is covered with the overall pattern of polka dots.	19th century.
29. Earthenware Coffee Pots.	The upper half has been dipped in a brown manganese glaze over a yellow clay.	Two whole pots.	The author, given by Mr John Roberts 2. One in Beacon, Collection in Whitehaven.	They are extremely well potted and glazed.	R.W. A rare mark impressed into the the clay under the handle.
30. Miniature toy Plate.	Willow (pale) blue/ white printed.	Whole pot plus a mass of shards.	Whitehaven pottery site.	Earthenware nicely potted and printed.	1820-40.
31. Small teapots	Moulded	Whole pots	The Dearham pottery	A treacle glaze. 1. The Mint Museum Carolina, USA. 3.The Helena Thompson Museum, Workington. 1. The author's purchased in a Cockermouth Antique shop. 1. Dr Frank Alpin Fort Worth, Texas U.S.A. (It was featured in the local 'Times and Star' newspaper in the 1970s).	Early 19th century.

TEAWARES OF THE WEST CUMBERLAND POTTERIES – *Continued*

OBJECT	PATTERN NAME	WHOLE POT/SHARD	ORIGIN	DESCRIPTION	MARK/DATE
32. Two Toddy Kettles.	Treacleglazed	Only two recorded.	Fox House Farm pottery. One owned by Miss Edith Turnbull and one by author.	Exceptionally well potted with a lovely glaze over a yellow clay body.	19th century.
33 Rum Butter Bowls	MARSEILLAISE also JAPAN pattern.	Whole pots and shards.	The Beacon Collection Whitehaven and local people also shards from the Whitehaven pottery site.	Family heirlooms used at local christenings. The rum butter is spread on cream crackers. This mixture kept the local ship wreckers alive whilst hiding in the caves along the coastline. The Japan pattern shards and a marked bowl have come to light only recently. These rum butter bowls were made at the Whitehaven pottery	1824-1915.
34 Tea sets	Blue and Green grass edged.	See 1814 Isle of Man advert. also shards illustrated in Volume I.	Whitehaven pottery site, See I.o.M. Gazette for 1819.	The shards were creamware, the I.o.M. advert for 1819 reads 'Supplied at the Whitehaven prices'.	1819 date of advertisement.
35. Tea sets	Printed Ware	Whole pots.	Shipping invoice dated 1836	L'dn size - 864 pieces Irish size 3,240 pieces Irish size 180 pieces shipped to U.S.A. to Mr John Dawson 26/2/1836	Invoice provided by Prof. George Miller and Asst. Prof. Dr Anne Smart-Martin, Winterthur University, U.S.A.

TEAWARES OF THE WEST CUMBERLAND POTTERIES – *Continued*

OBJECT	PATTERN NAME	WHOLE POT/SHARD	ORIGIN	DESCRIPTION	MARK/DATE
36. Tea sets	Painted ware	Whole teasets	Invoice of 1836	Ldn size unhandled 3,996 pieces	1836 –
37. Tea pots	Blackglazed Caneware	Whole pots Whole pots	Invoiced as above. Same invoice.	Iron oxide glaze 35 only 30 Teapots only.	1836
38. Coffee pots	Printed ware	Whole pots	Invoiced as above.	Printed ware 5 only	1836
39. Creamers	Painted ware Printed ware	Whole pots	Invoiced as above.	Painted ware 162 items Printed ware 114 items	1836.
40. Sugars	Painted ware	Whole pots	Invoiced as above.	Painted 10 only	1836
41. Muffins	Painted ware	Whole pots	Invoiced as above.	Painted ware 180 only	1836
42. Cream Ewers	Painted ware	Whole pots	Invoiced as above.	Painted ware 70 only.	1836
43. Lustreware Teasets.	Lustreware	Whole pots and shards.	Invoiced as above.	As advertised in 1814	1814
44. Three only unglazed teapots.	None	Nearly whole pots.	The Glass House pottery.	Mementos for the school which shared the same site as the Glass House pottery.	19th century.
45. A treacle glazed biscuit barrel.	Sprigged.	Whole pot.	The late Miss Edith Turnbull of Seaton, in West Cumberland.	Treacleglazed over a yellow clay body which had been sprigged.	19th century. Impressed on the reverse the potter's name John Docherty.
46. Part Bone China tea service	Engraving of Cockermouth Castle.	Whole pots and shards	Lady Egremont of Cockermouth Castle.	The teacups are the identical shape to the tea services made for St. Bees and Arlecdon Churches.	An underglaze back-stamp, black printed, with the name of the 'Sherwen Cockermouth'. In business on the Main Street in Cockermouth in the 1860s.

TEAWARES OF THE WEST CUMBERLAND POTTERIES – *Continued*

OBJECT	PATTERN NAME	WHOLE POT/SHARD	ORIGIN	DESCRIPTION	MARK/DATE
47. Spongeware teasets.	Earthenware in blue/white.	Shards only of teacup and saucers.	Excated on the Whitehaven Pottery site.	I would say Irish size.	These would be made for the early America market like the Marseillaise pattern cup with '9' shaped handle.

WHITEHAVEN POTTERY, DINNER WARES.

The early 21st century has seen a revolution in eating habits and so the demand for many ceramic items has declined. Many families no longer sit together around a dining table to enjoy a family meal.

Breakfast is usually a mug of tea or coffee, fruit juice or fresh fruit, porridge or cereal. However some men and woman neither eat or drink anything before going to work, but come 10am send for a *take away* coffee or tea, in a paper beaker and a bacon roll. Lunch is usually taken with their colleagues at a nearby café. Their evening meal consists of a snacked sandwich, then, they are off to the gym or in his wife's, or partner's case, to yoga!

Teatime paraphernalia i.e. the tea-set, cake-tazza, the large tea or coffee pot, and water jug are not quite obsolete but they are certainly not fashionable at the moment. However I must admit a visit to a good tea-shop which provides a nice china teapot (preferably white), which pours well, complete with tea strainer, and a jug of hot water together with a nice scone (still warm), butter, strawberry jam and cream, is undoubtedly a real treat.

At home in my china cabinet, I own a large soup tureen, together with a ladle and soup plates. I can boast 2 dinner services and 2 complete coffee services however I know many people who now use their best dinner plates for everyday use. Tureens are certainly obsolete. Coffee services have been replaced by mugs whilst soup is now mostly a lunchtime snack, usually served in a bowl. Hardly a family in the land now cooks a Sunday roast of beef, pork or lamb, except perhaps at Christmas.

Family occasions, anniversaries, birthdays etc., are mostly celebrated in a pub or hotel. People are not looking for work. Cooking, although enjoyed occasionally, becomes a chore if it is an everyday necessity. These days mothers with large families use mostly convenience food, which is readily available at their local supermarkets.

In the 19th century the Temperance Movement made us a nation of tea drinkers and this fashion was soon copied in the colonies i.e. Canada, Australia, New Zealand and the U.S.A. Today our children are copying the Americans by eating fast food usually

This large tureen and cover in the Mayfield pattern was featured in the True Blue Exhibition at the Wedgwood Museum in 1998, we have shards and marked items.

Eastern Scenery print please note the grape and vine inner border.

on a plate accompanied by a coke and curled up in front of the TV. In fact the famous Wedgwood factory has recently decided to manufacture supper trays with two wells, one for liquor, be it for a glass of milk, juice or a mug of tea, also one for the food, so if you can't beat them join them!.

Today's young women, don't like cleaning the family silver, so silver is no longer collectable; also she doesn't enjoy having to wash pots, so her crockery has to be dish washer proof, no more lovely gilded porcelain or bone china tea sets. Their expensive gold or platinum rims would disappear in her dish washer!

Then what is fashionable today? Since the introduction of Colour TV; colour in the home is very desirable. Therefore Clarice Cliff pots with their garish colours are in demand; as are small items, so that people can show them off in their cabinets. They are low maintenance. Cabinet plates, richly gilded and usually painted by the best artist of any given factory are expensive to buy but can be displayed easily in a nice cabinet.

The same can be said for Royal Doulton lady figurines or the Beswick factory figures. Rare old pieces will always be desired by Collectors. Plaques are low maintenance and are usually a work of art by the chosen artist of the factory.

Today's studio potters are trying their best to earn a living, hoping someone visiting his or her studio or gallery, will like this or that, and purchase the said item. Today's manufacturers are finding competition fierce; many have either closed shop or have been taken over by another manufacturer.

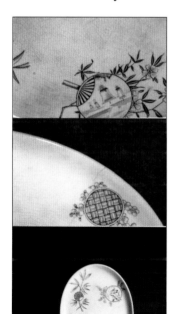

1. Khartoum Pattern on a small ashet, owned by a local person. Marked.

2. Marseillaise pattern.
a. top, shards and name
b. centre, flow blue shards
c. bottom, whole plate in a private collection.

3. Charity pattern owned by family of the late Rose McAllister.

Tureen and base in the Antiquities pattern, the Beacon Collection, Whitehaven.

The Lowther pattern identical to the Hillis Bowl. This plate is a sheet pattern and is unmarked however a 2nd plate is marked and features a border print.

The Minstrel pattern. This plate is also a sheet pattern, and shows the factory mark.

A Mayfield patterned plate, shards were excavated, see Volume I, showing pattern and initialls I.W. 1820.

A large brown/white ashet in the Asiatic Pheasant pattern, marked.

A Standard Willow plate, marked.

A tureen and ladle in the standard willow print, marked.

A large ashet. The centre panel is an underglaze print of the Bakers' Oven engraving. The border pattern is identical to the Whitehaven Pottery Lorretto, The Bottle and the Drunkards Doom series of plates on pages 88 and 89.

The Marseillaise print on this lovely drainer. Printed in underglaze brown/white.

Two dinner plates, (hardly used by the local family). The Marseillaise Print.

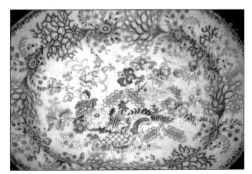

A large blue/white ashet in the Mayfield print.

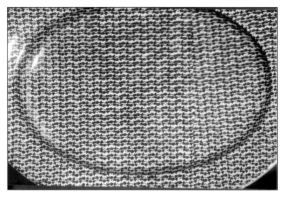

A sheet pattern ashet, the Peony pattern, courtesy of Wendy Mitton, Carlisle This large ashet is marked W.P.Co.

Dinner plate plus shards, in the Albion pattern.

John Wilkinson often lectured his work force on the misuse of alcohol and begged his men to abstain. Being a pious man he had poems or messages printed on his pots.

This plate 'The Drunkard's Doom' forms part of the Lindow Collection of Whitehaven pottery housed in the Beacon, Whitehaven. This print is also shown in The Bottle series of seven plates each showing a different print with the same border with an impressed star on the reverse.

The Bottle prints are taken from engravings by George Cruikshank (1840-50). See overleaf for further prints. This one is Scene Seven.

The border on this *The Bottle* and *Drunkards Doom* series of plates is identical to the Whitehaven pottery *Loretto* plate (see Volume I, page 53 Fig.) which depicts the print *Incident of our Blessed Saviour* also *The Baker's Oven* print which is illustrated on a large ashet on the previous page. They all depict the same impressed 'star' on the reverse.

Scene 3 has been illustrated by Noel Riley, page 265, No. 1055-1062, in her book *Gifts for Good Children* published by Richard Dennis, 1991. Noel Riley shows the plates which they think to be made by the Middlesborough Pottery, these display different aspects e.g. their border design, to our Whitehaven Factory.

These two plates depict the first and the second scenes *in this series of seven* 'The Bottle' *plates engraved by George Cruikshank, 1840-1850.*

Scene four *in this series and on the right hand side* scene five.

This is a scene six plate.   *Whitehaven pottery impressed* star mark *which is on many of their pots.*

Unfortunately I have not recorded a '*scene three*' of this series of seven engravings, see previously recorded comments regarding 'Scene Third' by Noel Riley on previous page.

A copper lustre jug which shows a policeman arresting a man, his wife and child are in the background. Courtesy of a local lady.

A small stoneware saltglazed bottle, which has been placed too near another bottle in the kiln.

At the Coronation of H.M. Queen Victoria, 28th June, 1838 the following appeared in the Cumberland Pacquet, 3/7/1838. Source, C.R.O. Carlisle.

The potters and pipemakers, 185 in number, joined together in the procession, they had three flags, one read Success to Commerce whilst on the reverse A View of the Pottery, another one read God Save The Queen. On the pipe-makers, a representation of 2 blacks smoking a pipe, (the armorial bearing of the trade), with this motto:- May brotherly Love Continue. Whilst on the reverse it reads God Save The Queen.

That morning 150 Potters were treated to breakfast by their esteemed master. The party sat down in front of the table, a bower, constructed by the workmen of flowers, evergreens, etc., which gave a very pleasant effect to the novel scene.

DINNERWARES MADE AT THE WHITEHAVEN POTTERY 1800-1915

OBJECT	PATTERN	COLOUR	WHOLE POT OR SHARD	ORIGIN	DESCRIPTION	DATE - MARK
1. Whole Dinner Service Large Drainer	MARSEILLIAISE A common pattern	Blue/White Green/White Flow Blue/ Brown/White Brown and White	Whole pots marked and shards.	Pottery site for shards. Whole Dinner Service bought by the Beacon Museum, Whitehaven at a local Auction Co. Author.	Earthenware, Underglaze printed Dinner Service contains three sizes of Dinner Plates, Tureens, Ashet and Sauce and Gravy boats.	IW made in 1820 Then JW stands for JOHN WILKINSON 1824-1868 under the glaze.
2. Tureens with Base	BOSPHORUS Uncommon Marked	Blue/White	Whole pots marked	The Beacon Collection Whitehaven	Trees, a tower, a lake with oriental type of sailing boats with men in them. Floral border, earthenware, under glaze printed.shows a man in the foreground with a hunting bird on his wrist.	IW made in 1820 Then JW stands for JOHN WILKINSON 1824-68 under the glaze.
3. Dinner Plates	CHARITY	Blue/White	Whole pots and shards.	Author's Collection and local people.	A lady is handing bread to children over a garden wall to two young children.	JW under the glaze 1824-68. This print is recorded by N. Riley Page 258 No. 1035 "Begging Arms".

DINNERWARES MADE AT THE WHITEHAVEN POTTERY 1800-1915 – Continued

OBJECT	PATTERN	COLOUR	WHOLE POT OR SHARD	ORIGIN	DESCRIPTION	DATE - MARK
4. A Dinner Plate	MINSTREL	Blue/White	Whole pot	Author's collection	A boy is playing his flute to a young girl with a dog. European type buildings in the background.	IW 1820-64 rare.
5. Tureen and Base	ANTIQUITIES.	Blue/White	Whole pots	Author's collection also one in the Beacon Collection, Whitehaven.	European ruins, also an oriental type of sailing boat with men in the foreground.	IW 1820.
6. Large Tureen also dinner plates and a small tureen base.	MAYFIELD	Blue/White	Whole pots and shards.	A large tureen was entered in The True Blue Exhibition at Barleston, Staffordshire.	Earthenware, under glaze printed in blue/white a floral print.	IW 1820.
7. Dinner plates, also a fruit bowl with moulded edge pips and a pickle dish	WILLOW	Blue/White	Whole pots and masses of shards from the pottery site.	Beacon Collection, author's collection and local people.	Earthenware, a Standard willow pattern which was exported in large amounts to the U.S.A. Ireland, and the Caribbean	IW 1820 and JW 1824-68 some pots also have the words "Warranted Semi China, and Stone China."
8. Large Ashet	FABRIC OR SHEET PATTERN	Blue/White	Whole pots	Mrs Wendy Mitton Carlisle.	Underglaze printed with small peonies.	W.P.Co. after 1872 After J. Wilkinson.

DINNERWARES MADE AT THE WHITEHAVEN POTTERY 1800-1915 – *Continued*

OBJECT	PATTERN	COLOUR	WHOLE POT OR SHARD	ORIGIN	DESCRIPTION	DATE - MARK
9. A set of blue sprigged jugs.	Semi China with blue sprigs.	White china body.	Whole pots.	The Beacon Collection.	Whitehaven Potteries contribution to the Asthetic movement-water jugs.	Wilkinson's Pottery Co., impressed in a circle under the pots therefore after 1872. These are rare.
10. Dinner Plates	LOWTHER	Blue/White.	Whole plates	Author's collection plus one is owned by a man in the South of Cumbria.	This is an identical print to the Hillis Bowl.	Marked W.& Co. impressed. Therefore before 1812-20 these are rare items.
11. Dinnerware	ASIATIC PHEASANTS	Blue/White, Green/White and Brown/White.	Whole pots.	Local antique shops in West Cumbria.	A common pattern used by many potteries in the U.K.	J.W. 1824-68. M. Wilkinson 1868-77.
12. Dinnerware	ALBION	Pale Blue/White.	Masses of shards on the Whitehaven Pottery site.	Author and many local people in West Cumbria.	A common pattern used by many potteries in the UK.	No marked items up to date.
13. A large ashet	EASTERN SCENERY	Blue/White under glaze printed.	Whole pot	Discovered in Brampton Antique centre.	Coysh and Henrywood *Dictionary of Blue and White Pottery* page 30, Irish Views; shows an identical border of grapes and vine leaf.	See Petra Williams Vol. II page, 172 for description of pattern, she dates 1818-46. Rare.

DINNERWARES MADE AT THE WHITEHAVEN POTTERY 1800-1915 – *Continued*

OBJECT	PATTERN	COLOUR	WHOLE POT OR SHARD	ORIGIN	DESCRIPTION	DATE - MARK
14. A Large ashet.	KARTOUN	Brown/White.	Whole pot.	Local farm people.	Whitehaven potteries attempting the Art Noveau style. It is very different.	1877-1915 W.P.Co. Whitehaven, the new owners trying something different.
15. Dinner plates.	Feather edged.	Blue and green edged.	Masses of shards.	Douglas Burn excavations by author and girls from St. Bees School in 1993. Also see advert in Isle of Man Gazette 1814 (by Eliz. Adams).	Creamware and earthenware shards showing the edges had been pressed with cockle shells on the plate outer rims to give the pattern.	Invoice, dated 1772 for creamware being sent to the U.S.A. provided by Prof. George Miller and Asst. Prof. Anne Smart Martin, Winterthur University, USA.
16. Dinner plates	Initialled in script "R.D." with hand painted sprigs of foliage around the rim.	Blue/White.	Whole pots.	Two east Cumbrian ladies brought them to the N.C.S. Summer school at Chester in 2004.	Pearlware, the centre of the two plates initialled "R.D." surrounded with a shamrock, rose and thistle.	One plate is impressed W. & Co., and the other Woodnorth & Co. 1812-20. Rare.
17. Dinner plate.	The signature of James Brindley the Staffordshire Engraver can be seen in the grass. It is very rare.	Black and White Printed with a black rim	Whole pot.	Recorded by Dr. G. Godden in his *Encyclopia of Pottery and Porcelain Marks in the Appendix.* Page 33.	I was given the negative of the photograph of this plate by the late Mr. Frank Hendren, Whitehaven.	The date is on the milestone 1819. Dr. G. Godden records this plate to be in the Bethnal Green Museum, Ldn, now mislaid.

WHITEHAVEN POTTERY, KITCHENWARES

Please let your imagination go back to the time when labour was cheap, and everything accountable, and valued in the kitchen where Cook was in charge.

A visit to the Beamish Museum in the north east, or the kitchens of nearby Raby Castle or even closer to home the Millom Folk Museum gives one some idea of the great number and variety of pots which were being used in these kitchens. Kitchenware, through necessity has been created by potters over the centuries. These vessels were used to hold food and liquid for the poor people whilst the rich had silver, pewter and even turned wood flatwares. Large crocks were produced so that eggs could be immersed in isinglass in order to sustain a family throughout the winter months and large bowls in which cook or mother would kneed her bread dough, then let it rest and rise, covered with a cloth by the fire until it was ready to be put in the oven. These large bowls were usually made of a coarse brown earthenware with a slipt white glazed interior and part slipt on the outside. Mother's willow patterned mixing bowl held her ingredients for either cakes or biscuits whilst the sometimes smaller banded ware bowls held her separate ingredients. Today these are now highly sought after and fashionable.

Shards of banded and Mocha Ware depicting the worm pattern.

Jug and bowl set with a moulded neck. The blue/white print is the sheet 'Peony Pattern'.

There would be large stoneware jars as described in the Isle of Man. newspaper advertisement in 1814 which I have recorded on a previous page; it records half gallon to five gallon jars being offered for sale, by the Whitehaven factory. These held the precious oil for the lamps, (no gas or electricity then). They also made thousands of plant pots for use in the garden and large jardinières to display the family aspidistra; also candle holders and stone hot water bottles for bedtime.

Mantle ornaments were a popular item, these showed off the newly polished and black leaded fireplace. Plumbing was very primitive in these times, so hot and cold water was carried long distances, both for consumption and hygiene purposes, so large water jugs were the order of the day.

Breakfast usually consisted of a bowl of porridge, so large milk jugs would be required, and mugs. Then there were the fruit dishes to display the fruit in season, be it apples, pears or the soft fruit like gooseberries, strawberries or raspberries together with the attractive hand painted bowls for bulbs or plants, in the Persian Rose design which is still popular today.

A Tongue Press.

One of my mentors during my thirty or so years of researching the Cumbria pot banks has been Peter Brears. Now advisor to English Heritage on stonewares and country pottery. His book on '*Country Potters*' lit my candle, and has kept it glowing all these years. It was a great privilege to meet up with him for the first time at the 2004 N.C.S. Summer School at Chester University.

Peter Brears told me about the Whitehaven pottery Tongue Press housed in the Isle of Man Museum which I illustrate above. Pressed tongue was a local Cumbria delicacy, together with cooked ham and salad which was served at every local wedding, christening or funeral at this time and invariably held in the local Co-operative Hall. A menu that was presented until well into the 1950s.

I immediately put in a request for a photograph and courtesy of Mr Richardson of the Manx National Museum, Manx Heritage, Douglas; I.o.M. this rare pot (for few have survived) can now be illustrated in this book.

The tongue press consists of a series of tiered earthenware ceramic rings. As the Cook carves the tongue, a ring is taken off. My mother 'pressed her cow's tongues' using gelatine, then the whole, was weighted down with an iron, or any other heavy object to hand, until they had set.

Pair of Marseillaise pattern large jugs, the one on the left is printed in green, whilst the centre jug is printed in blue and white.

A large jug printed in the Bosphorus pattern in brown/white.

Large jug in the Charity pattern.

A fruit bowl in the Bosphorus pattern.

Cereal bowl which illustrates the sponging technique of decoration.

Large jardinière (a second) the base is burnt!

Large crock pot. Iron oxide glazed.

Large stoneware jar.

Mantle ornaments, in the biscuit stage, rescued from the Whitehaven pottery by the Lowther Estates staff when the site was sold.

Pair of hand painted bowls in the Persian rose design.

A large bread/broth bowl.

The treacle jar on the left is illustrated courtesy of Mrs Barbara Blenkinship. The border print is identical to that on the reverse of the Bosporus fruit bowl. The jar to the right is courtesy of Joyce Cockerill, 12th Dec., 1992. (Treacle was a by-product of the refining of sugar at Whitehaven).

KITCHENWARE

OBJECT	PATTERN NAME	WHOLE POT OR SHARD	ORIGIN	DESCRIPTION	DATE MADE
1. Treacle jar.	Usually blue/white and underglaze printed.	Whole pot also shards from the Whitehaven pottery site.	Family heirlooms. Whitehaven imported sugar from the Caribbean. Every local household had it's Treacle jar so mother made ginger bread and Mint Balls.	Usually a flask with a screw lid and flora and fauna prints of children.	1824-68 unmarked family heirlooms.
2.Stoneware hot water bottles.	Usually one half is split whilst the rest remains brown.	Whole pots. Common.	Local.	Poor families used firebricks with a towel around it whilst others went to bed on a cold night hugging their water bottle.	1868-77.
3. Mantle ornaments.	Treacle glazed or hand painted either plain or with double twist handles or sprigged with moulded items of flora and fauna.	Whole pots whilst others are not quite finished – brought from the Lowther family Estate Office in Whitehaven and handed to the then Museum Curator.	The Beacon Collection and local families.	Approx. 18-20" tall they would stand on each side of a coal fired grate. The finer pots would decorate the parlour.	1840-1915.
4. Bowls for Cooking.	Banded ware, mocha and yellow ware (domestic pots).	Whole pots and masses of shards.	These shards were excavated from Whitehaven, Clifton and Fox House Farm site.	The shards showed the colours hardened on. Whole pots with circles of slip around them.	1840.

KITCHENWARE – *Continued*

OBJECT	PATTERN NAME	WHOLE POT OR SHARD	ORIGIN	DESCRIPTION	DATE MADE
5. Dipped ware.	Brown earthenware.	Whole pots and shards.	Shipping invoice.	Half the pot would have been dipped into a liquid slip. The turned section would have various colours painted and hardened on.	1836 date of invoice to U.S.A.
6. Bread Crocks.	Coarse earthenware glazed on the outside only – plain no décor.	Whole pots and masses of shards.	Excavated from most sites.	Usually a red clay, slipt inside where dribbling appears.	1820-1915.
7. Salters.	Brosely and Willow	Whole pots and shards.	The Whitehaven pottery.	They resemble an egg cup.	1824-1915.
8. Furniture rests.	To keep the items of furniture off the damp flagged floor.	Whole pots.	The Pitblade family of Whitehaven. Their ancestor was the potter at the Ginns House pottery.	Usually sold in sets of four.	1840.
9. Large Water Jugs.	Peony and Marseillaise. Date 1824-68.	Whole pots.	Local people.	Underglaze printed approx. 20″ in height. The Whitehaven pottery.	Peony pattern W.P.Co. 1890
10. Candle Holder.	Agate.	Whole pots.	From the Kitchin family who owned the Ginns House Pottery, Whn.	Brown and Yellow clays are kneaded then glazed.	1840.
11. Cooking pots or tatiepot dishes.	Usually plain brown.	Whole pots and masses of shards.	Local families.	Earthenware, glazed lug handles.	1754-1915 The Ginns House, Fox House and Clifton.

WHITEHAVEN POTTERY, MISCELLANEOUS WARE

Whitehaven was second to London, as far as records go with regards to the shipping trade. Great sailing ships were built here which sailed to the Americas, the Far East and the Baltic, and imported vast quantities of tobacco leaf, sugar and hard wood. Thomas and Joseph Brocklebank, were born in Whitehaven, their father being Daniel. They merged with the Liverpool based Cunard shipping line and became the freight arm of the company.

The two sailing ships illustrated above were built in Whitehaven. The ship on the left was named The Aracan the one on the right was named The Silverhow.

In the late 18th and early 19th century life was a dreadful existence for all seamen. Some had not had a pay rise since the days of Oliver Cromwell. It was no wonder some of these men who had not been paid for say 18 months, decided *enough was enough.*

Their conditions were claustrophobic. By 1797 these seamen decided to mutiny perhaps hearing of the Free Ireland Movement or the French Revolution they decided to fight back. The parliament of the day relented and decreed their pay and conditions be improved.

In the Beacon Collection, Whitehaven, we are fortunate to have a large Admiral Duncan creamware ale jug.* The inscription congratulates him on his famous victory at Camperdown against the Dutch navy which was under Admiral De Winter. Duncan was one of our four most famous naval officers in history. The other three being Lord Nelson, John Earl St. Peter, and Richard Earl Howe.

Admiral Duncan is also associated and given credit for peacefully quelling a mutiny in the British Navy, whilst one of his young able seaman, John Crawford of Sunderland, is said to have nailed back his ship's colours, (the Venerable's flag) after it had been blasted off by the cannons of the Dutch Admiral De Winter's ship. In other words he was telling the enemy nailing the flag to what was left of his ship's mast *we shall fight to the last man.* Unfortunately Duncan's victory was soon overshadowed by Nelson's glorious successes in the battles of the Nile and then Trafalgar.

---

* *See Chapter 1.*

The Whitehaven Harbour at this period would resemble *Gulliver's Shoes* with the hustle and bustle of working men. Joiners banging away as we say in Cumbria. Incoming Clippers being off loaded then loaded. Coal was being loaded onto ships going to Ireland, the Isle of Man and southern Scotland and even to the Americas. The coal came from the Earl of Lonsdale's local coal mines via a wagon-way which entered the harbour via the town centre from a nearby goods siding. On the northern entrance to the town, wagons filled with coal came into the harbour directly from his many small coal mines situated on the outskirts of the borough.

The Earl of Lonsdale and the local ship owners commissioned artists from the local marine school of art to paint the great sailing ships, in full sail off our piers. Especially as the Solway coastline is renowned for its sunsets. A lot of these wonderful paintings are on view in the Liverpool Maritime Museum.

All this activity created great wealth and an abundance of opportunity for local entrepreneurs.

Most evenings these workmen enjoyed their pints and their clay pipes. Today's doctors relate most men's health problems to the lack of proper exercise and a need to quench a thirst. At this period of time men worked hard, doing physical jobs, be it in mining, shipping or on the land. Their thirsts were quenched by drinking a pint mug of tea or beer, or a jug of cider, the containers being produced by the local potteries.

Fun items were made for example Frog Mugs or Loving Cups which held a sculptured frog in the bottom. I often boast that our Cumbria frogs are superior to their

Three Whitehaven pottery puzzle jugs.
The one on the left is the Charity pattern. Centre jug depicts the Fruit pattern whilst the one of the right hand side, which is broken, is a Flora and fauna print. Please note the different forms of piercing through which the liquid flows over the unsuspecting victim of a public house wager.

A moulded log shaped Hot Water
Bottle and rare impressed mark
R. WILKINSON, WHITEHAVEN

Staffordshire or North East counterparts!

Men like to wager, so most evenings, out would come an Inn Keeper's Puzzle Jug. Being the owner, he was aware of which particular hole to hold one's finger over to make it airtight. The unsuspecting miner or seafarer did not, hence the wager, so to the delight of the onlookers the contents, usually ale, would finish up all over the victim's trousers!

Money boxes were also produced, encouraged by John Wilkinson, who explained to his work force that it was *good to save their hard earned money.*

Bachelor sets, comprised a series of objects which fitted one on top of the other and were really a culmination of all the foul habits of this era.

They are topped with a candle stick, next comes a goblet, underneath the goblet is the tobacco jar then a chamber pot and lastly a spitoon!

Money boxes donated by the Sloan Family of Whitehaven, centre border is depicted on a tobacco jar below whilst the one on the left is on the Isle of Man milk jug, (see Teawares, page 64). In the Beacon Collection.

Tobacco Jar, dated 1853 owned by Wendy Mitton, Antique dealer, Carlisle.

A tobacco jar in the Charity pattern, courtesy of Wendy Mitton, Carlisle.

A baby's feeding bottle, in the Moss Rose pattern. This pattern was also printed by Messrs Mintons. Shards were excavated.

A Batchelor's outfit housed in the Beacon Collection, Whitehaven.	*A blue/white tobacco jar signed S.D. 1851, courtesy of Mrs Charles Humphreys Senior, Whitehaven. In the Beacon Collection. Whitehaven.*	*Soft paste porcelain tobacco jar recognised by Tom Walford, the Editor of the E.C.C. Journal; it is housed in the Nottingham Castle Museum.*

Garden Furniture   *The T.P. Attwood plaque.*
This item of garden furniture is owned by Mrs Wendy Mitton of Carlisle, one similar was shown to me by the late Ida Parrish (local historian)Whitehaven, in the 1980s.

The Batchelor's Set illustrated on page 104 was donated by David Whitaker's mother, 60 years ago to the then Whitehaven Museum. Luckily we have a second Batchelor's Set in the Beacon Collection, in Whitehaven. These are rare items.

After the Reform Act of 1832 (*see Daniel Hay An Illustrated History of Whitehaven,* page 196, for an explanation). Mathias Attwood, a Birmingham banker contested the Whitehaven parliamentary constituency in 1832, in the Lowther interest. His reform opponent Isaac Littledale was a member of a prominent Whitehaven family and owned

A pearlware beaker inscribed and dated.

One of these recently fetched £850 plus VAT at a local auction.

the Lowca Chemical and Tar Works, a couple of miles north of the town. Attwood won 211, votes to Littledale 173.

We have in the Beacon collection a number of pots displaying the Free Trade Print which I have illustrated whilst others are family heirlooms. Note the identical print on our Whitehaven Pottery shaving boxes. I illustrate one in black/white and one in sepia, in the Toilet ware section. The same border print can be seen on the Isaac Sloan bequest money boxes and on Wendy Mitton's charity pattern tobacco jar, also the charity pattern puzzle jug in The Beacon Collection. I have also recorded clobbered items in these vivid red, green and blue high temperature enamels. The Loving Cup and One Pint Mug in the article on the right show our Whitehaven pottery borders.

"COMMEMORATIVE POTTERY 1780–1900"   John & Jennifer May page 150. pub. 1972

225. An unusual print published by the Anti-Corn-Law League: this particular mug is of peculiar interest because it has a frog in it. Commemorative frog mugs are rare.

226. Another unusual transfer recommending the repeal of the Corn Laws and the cause of free trade: this is printed in blue on this very impressive loving cup, and is the only example of the transfer so far recorded.

"No monopoly" and "Free Trade". In the immediate foreground several mice are nibbling holes in a tract encaptioned "corn law".

Both these transfers may be printed in brown or black, and both are usually overglaze-'clobbered' in a fairly vivid palette.

(c) A very much rarer transfer, so far encountered only on a 13.75cm plate, printed in black and overglaze-enamelled, shows a ship just breaking out her sails as she leaves harbour; a pile of cargo stands on the harbour wall. Above, the print is encaptioned, "Commerce"; and below, "The Staffordshire potteries and free trade with all nations".

(d) Another rare print, again only met with so far on a plate, 15.00cm diameter, black-printed and overglaze-clobbered, shows a ship sailing into harbour, its sails embellished with the slogan "Free Trade". The print is encaptioned, over the scene, "Free trade with all nations".

(e) A print very similar to the last described shows an apparently identical ship entering a harbour, with in the foreground, a warehouse into which a number of barrels of flour are being loaded. The print is encaptioned "Manufactures in exchange for corn".

(f) This is teamed, on the only piece on which either of the transfers have so far been seen (a blue and white loving cup, 15.00cm high by 11.25cm diameter), with a similar ship, also flying the flag of "Free Trade" lying off shore, while in the foreground Britannia, scroll in hand, discusses a treaty of trade with the 'four continents' expressed in allegoric style. The print is encaptioned "Free trade with all the world".

(g) Last, and perhaps one of the most interesting pieces of the whole Corn Law saga, is a plate commemorating not one of the great heroes but the comparatively minor orator and writer, Colonel Perronet Thompson.

The plate, which is 17.5cm diameter, very poorly printed in black and with a coarse daisy border, shows the Colonel, with his prominent kiss-curl of hair, glowering formidably from a head-and-shoulders portrait. The print is encaptioned simply "Colonel Thompson".

The cause of the Free Trade campaign and/or the celebra-

The above article on Free Trade was written by Jonathan and Jennifer May, page 150 of their book published in 1972, on 'Commemorative Pottery, 1780-1860'.

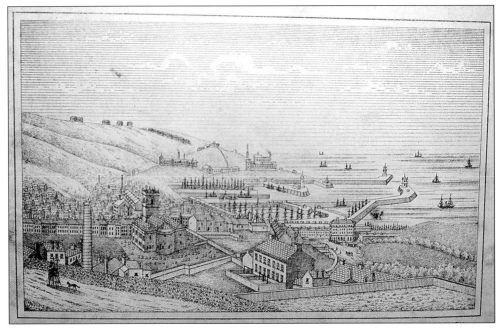

An early nineteenth century print of Whitehaven and the harbour taken from Wellington Row which is to the north of the town. Within the harbour and outside the pier at least 50 sailing ships can be counted.

Mr and Mrs Moses Kennedy, antique dealers outside their shop in the Market Place, Whitehaven. This photograph was given to me by Mrs McGrady who also owned a shop in the Market Place. She was a friend of my grandmother, Mrs Laura Trevaskis.

POTS MADE AT THE WEST CUMBERLAND POTTERIES – MISCELLANEOUS

OBJECT	PATTERN	WHOLE POT OR SHARD	ORIGIN	DESCRIPTION	MARK OR DATE
1. Smoker's Sets comprising a. Candlestick b. Wine Goblet c. Tobacco Jar d. Chamber pot e. Spittoon	Usually black and white underglaze printed in the Marseillaise print.	Two nearly complete sets have been presented to the Whitehaven Museum.	Local people	Earthenware approx. 3 feet in height when assembled	Unmarked, however the pattern on them is Marseillaise which is a common Whitehaven Pottery pattern 1820-40.
2. Darning Eggs and bell/curtain pulls.	The egg prints usually depicts a child whilst the bell/curtain pulls are botanical prints.	Mainly whole pots however shards of The Kite and Charity prints were excavated on the site in the 1980s.	Four Darning eggs are in the Beacon Collection Whitehaven. A bell/curtain pull holds back the drapes surrounding Queen Victoria's bed at Osborne house on the Isle of Wight.	Early eggs are bat printed. The Darning eggs are underglaze printed horizontally whilst the bell curtain pulls are printed vertically. Many are named or initialled with one exception; there is a blue sponged egg in the Beacon collection.	Unmarked however the local people (owners) report the names to be members of their family. These are rare items. Usually family heirlooms 1820-40.
3. Character Jugs	Treacleglazed depicting Aly Sloper reported to have had a large nose.	Whole pot. These jugs have been reported in lead and cast iron. This is unique up to date.	Local man whose father was a good friend of the potter.	Earthenware.	From the Clay Flatts pottery, The Marsh, Workington, made by Jonnie Dunbar who also worked at Fox House Farm pottery 1840.
4. Babies feeding bottles	Moss Rose pattern flora-fauna, base smear glazed.	Whole pots and shards in blue/white and brown/white.	Beacon collection and local people.	Flat in shape, earthenware underglaze printed.	Whitehaven pottery 1820-1915.

POTS MADE AT THE WEST CUMBERLAND POTTERIES – MISCELLANEOUS – *Continued*

OBJECT	PATTERN	WHOLE POT OR SHARD	ORIGIN	DESCRIPTION	MARK OR DATE
5. Plant pots		Masses of shards on every pottery site.	Local pottery sites and local people.	Made from a very red clay, usually they display an iron oxide glaze or are unglazed.	1820-1915 Whitehaven, Ginns, Clifton, Fox House Farm and others.
6. Religious and presentation plates	Loretto – religious scenes sending out a message e.g. Band of Hope also Drunkards Doom print.	Whole pots	The Beacon collection plus local people.	These and The Bakers Oven print share the same border print.	Presentation plate inscribed to the landlord of a local hostelry and has the Marseillaise border print.
7. Tobacco Jars	Hand painted in blue/white.	Whole pots	Local families. Beacon Collection and family heirlooms.	Usually named.Volume I I illustrate an earthenware brown glazed initialled and dated tobacco jar.	Initialled I.M. and dated 1791 the year Rev. John Wesley died. This date is also recorded on the Rev. John Fletcher Children's plates.
8. Plates	Tortoiseshell glazed	Shards only	Whitehaven pottery site dig in 1983 reported in the NCS Newsletter.	A light clay under body, moulded border, tortoiseshell glazed.	1820-40
9. Spirit Flasks	One is Treacleglazed. One shows a yellow clay body which is glazed and blue sprigged. One shows the young head of H.M. Queen Victoria.	Whole pots	Thought to have been boot warmers but now recorded by the experts as spirit flasks. The blue sprigged flask is in The Beacon Collection.	The treacleglazed spirit flask was given to the Helena Thompson Museum, Workington by the author. The Beacon recorded the sprigged flask was made at the Ladypit pottery – a rare item.	1840-72 both are unmarked. The treacleglazed pot came from the Netherhall Estate, Maryport.

POTS MADE AT THE WEST CUMBERLAND POTTERIES – MISCELLANEOUS – *Continued*

OBJECT	PATTERN	WHOLE POT OR SHARD	ORIGIN	DESCRIPTION	MARK OR DATE
10. Coronation Mugs	Blue/white inscribed	Whole pots	Given to pupils of The Glass House School in the Ginns – they were made to commemorate the coronation of H.M. Queen Victoria in 1838.	Earthenware, half pint in size, inscribed. One recently sold for £850 plus at Mitchells Auction Rooms in Cockermouth.	Dated 1838.
11. Frog Mugs	Free Trade print or Flora and Fauna blue/white printed. One is initialled W.D.	Whole pots and shards from pottery site.	The Beacon Collection, Whitehaven and local people and author's collection.	Inscribed, usually blue/white underglaze printed Eatheware, however there are some black/white printed pots showing the Free Trade print. The frogs are well moulded – fun items.	1820-72.
12. Puzzle Jugs	Charity pattern also Flora and fauna, or brown glazed.	Whole pots, usually marked.	The Beacon Collection and local people. Usually family heirlooms.	Fun items often demonstrated by the experts on the various T.V. programmes. By putting one's fingers over the correct nozzle it is possible to create a vacuum enabling the owner to suck out the contents. However, the unsuspecting sailor or miner getting it wrong gets the ale over his trousers!	1820-72 onwards.
13. A moulded hot water bottle	The spout has a petalled flower surrounding it.	Whole pot.	Bought by the owner from a dealer.	Brown and white slipped stoneware resembles a log.	Impressed name R. WILKINSON, WHITEHAVEN a rare mark.

POTS MADE AT THE WEST CUMBERLAND POTTERIES – MISCELLANEOUS – Continued

OBJECT	PATTERN	WHOLE POT OR SHARD	ORIGIN	DESCRIPTION	MARK OR DATE
14. Money Boxes	They show the Free Trade print on those made for the grown ups. Those for children are made of coarse earthenware and slip decorated.	Whole pots and shards.	Isaac Sloan bequest in the Beacon Collection. The children's boxes belong to local people.	Earthernware usually under glaze printed. The children's boxes are usually broken where the coins come out.	1820-72. Made at the Whitehaven pottery. Whilst the children's boxes were made at Fox House Farm, Great Broughton.
15. Political Items	Inscribed	Whole pots and shards.	In various Museums e.g. The Beacon Whitehaven, Brighton Museum local people and author.	A cripsly moulded shard excavated at the Fox House Farm pottery at Broughton Moor shows a moulding (part of a Tureen Lid) which depicts two large crossed keys so obviously it was being made for the House of Keys, Isle of Man. There are also the inscribed Reform Bill Pearlware Beakers.	Inscribed 1832.
16. Slipware Dishes	The Royal Arms	Two of these large dishes are inscribed.	1. 'Clifton Dish' found by the author aprox. 1989 in a farmhouse at Crossbarrow, Clifton.	These three dishes are very important items in the history of ceramics in Cumberland.	The Clifton Dish is now thought to be have been made for a local marriage by James Tunstall a local potter who used the Stephen Shaw mould. *Continued overleaf*

POTS MADE AT THE WEST CUMBERLAND POTTERIES – MISCELLANEOUS – *Continued*

OBJECT	PATTERN	WHOLE POT OR SHARD	ORIGIN	DESCRIPTION	MARK OR DATE
16. Slipware Dishes – *Continued*			2. The Fitzwilliam Museum Dish discovered by Messrs Phillips, London when the Clifton Dish was to be auctioned. 3. The British Museum Dish from the same mould discovered by the experts is inscribed 'By Stephen Shaw 1725' on the reverse.		Stephen Shaw ex Staffordshire potter signed the dish discovered in the British Museum on the reverse By Stephen Shaw, 1712. The Clifton Dish is signed on the reverse 'Clifton Dish'.
17. A third large ale Jug in creamware.	Made for a local Masonic Lodge.	Whole pot but printed Shards were excavated.	The Beacon Collection houses two and the 119 Lodge in Whitehaven the third large jug.	One is inscribed for a Local Mariner Daniel McIntosh. A second is inscribed to the Cordwainers Society. Whilst the third is Decorated with Masonic symbols.	The jugs are the oldest in our Collection of Whitehaven Creamware and very important items of early 19th century pottery.

WHITEHAVEN POTTERY, TOILET WARES

Dealing with this category made me realise how lucky we are not to be living a century ago. We no longer allow the filthy habits which were permitted then. Someone had to empty those chamber pots, ash trays and spittoons! Someone had to carry the buckets and large jugs of hot water to the bedrooms for their master or mistress and someone had to get rid of the contents of the dry toilets!

The Doctors had their bleeding bowls, whilst gentlemen had their shaving bowls. Thank heavens for progress i.e. showers and baths, flush toilets, electric shavers and ensuite accommodation. Yes we have made great improvements to our well being, both in health and hygiene.

Pagoda pattern, this is a unique jug and bowl set, courtesy of the Friends of the Edward Hornel Museum Broughton House, Kirkcudbrightshire (1982). Now owned by the Scottish National Trust.

Please note the grape and vine border on the inside of this bowl. This border is on the Eastern Scenery and Bosphorus patterns i.e. a large blue/white ashet and b/w fruit bowl.

The border pattern shows boys in oriental type clothes, flying a kite.

A BOSPHORUS pattern bowl showing mark, pattern name, and initials (I.W.) also the grape and vine border as on the Eastern Scenery and the Pagoda patterns.

BOSPHORUS pattern jug and bowl set.

MARSEILLAISE pattern, a tooth brush holder.

A CHARITY pattern bowl.

A shaving bowl printed in underglaze black/white of the 'Free Trade in exchange for Corn'.
Courtesy of the Isaac Sloan family, Whitehaven.

Gentleman's shaving bowl and lid, note the words 'Free Trade in exchange for Corn.' which surround the lid, printed in sepia.
Courtesy of Mrs Barbara Blenkinship, Penrith.

TOILET WARES MADE AT THE WEST CUMBERLAND POTTERIES

OBJECT	PATTERN NAME	WHOLE POT OR SHARD	ORIGIN	DESCRIPTION	DATE/MARK
1. The Hillis Bowl	LOWTHER the name was invented by the author.	Whole objects	Dr. Maurice Hillis	This large bowl was reported in the NCS quarterly newsletter issue No. 16 March, 1990. Printed in black with added high temperature colours in a Pratt type palette i.e blue green, yellow and orange.	W.H.H. WHITEHAVEN which stands for Woodnorth, Harrison and Hall the founders of the Whitehaven Pottery 1812-1820. These are rare items.
2. Jug and Bowl Set.	BOSPHORUS uncommon	Whole pots and shards.	The Beacon Collection, Whitehaven, also the Edward Hornel Museum and Art Gallery, Kirkcudbrightshire which is now owned by the Scottish National Trust.	In the foreground are two men, one holds a falcon on his wrist. There is a European type of Palace in the background and a back drop of mountains with trees. It has a floral border with trellis on a blue wash.	Marked J.W. John Wilkinson 1824-68.
3. Jug and Bowl Set	MARSEILLAISE A misspelling by the Whitehaven, potter, it should read Marseilles a port in France.	Whole pots and shards	The Beacon Collection Whitehaven; also local people own items in this pattern	Underglaze printed in a palette of blue, green and brown on earthenware. It usually depicts various sailors with their ladies or a lady. The sailor is usually holding a telescope to his eye. The rare version of this pattern shows a woman in a long dress holding the hands of children.	I.W. 1820 J.W. 1824-68 most pieces are marked.

Continued on next page

114

TOILET WARES MADE AT THE WEST CUMBERLAND POTTERIES – *Continued*

OBJECT	PATTERN NAME	WHOLE POT OR SHARD	ORIGIN	DESCRIPTION	DATE/MARK
4. Tooth Brush holder.	MARSEILLAISE	Whole pot and shards	The Beacon Collection, Whitehaven	Printed in blue and white under the glaze.	J.W. 1824-68 John Wilkinson A rare object.
5. Men's shaving bowls	FREE TRADE Also two mugs in coarse earthenware	Whole pots some initialled and dated	The Beacon Whitehaven. Recently a mug fetched £380s plus.	Printed in underglaze black/white. Donated by the Isaac Sloan family, Whitehaven.	J.W. 1824-68 John Wilkinson The coarse earthen ware mugs probably made by J. Tunstall.
6. Jug and Bowl set	PAGODA	Whole pot	Edward Hornel Art Gallery and Museum in Kirkcudbrightshire now owned by the Scottish National Trust	This is my favourite piece of Whitehaven pottery. A Mandarin with his lady is being punted, in an oriental type boat with a carved dragon figurehead, earthenware and underglaze printed in blue/white. The border depicts two children flying their kites in cartouches. Between the centre print on the inside of the bowl and the border print there is a trailing vine with grapes and foliage.	J.W. 1824-68 marked on the reverse. An extremely rare item.
7. Jug and bowl set.	CHARITY	Whole pots and shards	The Beacon Collection Whitehaven	This pattern is to be found on the Whitehaven pottery puzzle jugs etc.	I.W. 1820 J.W. 1824-68 Marked on the reverse.

Misspellings by the Whitehaven Potters:-

Marseilles   Is a port in the south of France, the romanticised scene captured on the Whitehaven pots of this period 1824-1868. However, the Whitehaven engraver has spelt it Marseillaise which is the name of the French National Anthem..

Daughter   Whitehaven Potters have spelt it Doter.

Kartoum   Kartoun.

Peking   Pekin.

Nanking   Nankin.

St. Bees Church and College – The early creamware pots describe the scene as Cottage, however, this was later changed to College.

WHITEHAVEN POTTERY, CHILDREN'S PLATES.

These small plates would be the *bread and butter* of the Whitehaven factory, they are *cheap and cheerful*, a useful present for any christening or birthday. West Cumberland and Ireland (their main market) had a high birth rate and mortality rate at this period.

Northern Ceramic Society Newsletter No. 118, June, 2000, pages 21 and 22, I recorded and illustrated a number of excavated shards depicting children at play, consequently in 2004 when my husband and I purchased a copy of Noel Riley's book *Gifts for Good Children*, at the Stoke Ceramics Museum in Hanley, Staffordshire, you can imagine our surprise to find children's plates depicting identical prints to those on our Whitehaven pottery darning eggs which are unique to this factory. The North East potteries made the much smaller hen eggs which they sold as *hand warmers*.

Fortunately, shortly after this, we visited the N.E.C. Antiques Fair at Birmingham where we purchased three small Whitehaven pottery creamware plates. The centre prints on these plates are *The Romp, Keeping School and Now I'm Grandmother*. All three prints show the same border, hand painted sprays of foliage, in vivid enamel colours of red, green and blue, over the glaze.

When we arrived home we noted Noel Riley illustrates a forth plate showing the same border and named *The Young Charioteer*. I had recorded shards depicting this print in the N.C.S. Newsletter of June 2000 as being underglaze printed *in a variety of colours*.

That same day the author purchased a small child's plate inscribed *Beggars Petition* in earthenware. Once again I had reported excavating a large fire damaged shard in a previously published edition of the Northern Ceramic Society Newsletter. The print is underglaze black/white printed with a moulded rim of hanging garlands of flowers interspersed with bouquets of flowers. There are two black printed inner and outer rim circles which surround the centre print. The plate has a scalloped edge. The plate looks rather greyish in colour supporting the claim that the Whitehaven pottery is now starting to use bone ash in their earthenware body.

Summer 2005 a Welsh ceramist approached me at the N.C.S. Seminar at Chester University. He had brought a small plate to show me. The moulded border had the same hanging garlands of flowers as on the border of *The Beggar's Petition* plate made at the Whitehaven factory, however on his plate, at the end of each hanging garland of flowers was a hanging bunch of grapes. This added moulding was much crisper than the moulded garlands of flowers, which made me think this was not the original moulding. The centre print was in an imari style, very colourful, not like anything I have seen up to date on a Whitehaven pot.

My reaction was to tell him that I thought this plate had been made at the Glamorgan pottery from a Whitehaven mould which had been modified. However they had used a Glamorgan print for the centre of the plate.

A creamware plate printed with Keeping School.

A creamware plate printed.
Now I'm Grandmother.

Creamware plate printed with The Romp.

Children's pots, showing The Romp print on a small plate, also a darning egg and a mug. A second plate shows the Keeping School print whilst a frog mug depicts the same. These were all made at Whitehaven.

A small creamware plate and a child's mug purchased at the 2004 Birmingham N.E.C. Fair. They depict The Beggar's Petition print. The plate is printed in pink. A second plate depicting this print is illustrated on the right hand side; it shows a greyness of the earthenware body. Between the plates is an excavated fire damaged shard, printed in sepia, from the Whitehaven pottery site.

The author came home from the same N.E.C. Birmingham Fair in 2005 with a creamware child's plate depicting the Little Titty print (another darning egg print). This time printed in underglaze green, proving the Whitehaven potters are experimenting with colour. The above plates show the same border moulding of rose, tulip and aster however please note on the Feeding Her Chickens *plate the moulding has been painted over in vivid blue, green and red enamels.*

An earthenware plate of the Little Titty print. The border is the fish scale moulding.
Courtesy of Mrs Barbara Blenkinship.

Shard showing the fish scale moulding in biscuit, with a colour hardened on, from the Whitehaven pottery site.

The following is a small child's mug which was also purchased at the Birmingham Antiques Fair. It depicts the *Beggar's Petition* print however we then discovered the reverse showed a print *unrecorded up to date The First Nibble* for which we had various excavated shards. The sepia shards show a small boy fishing, whilst 2 young girls watch him. The blue and white shards show part of a boy's hand which is holding what appears to be a stick however we now know it is a fishing line. The Whitehaven factory had the print over painted with vivid green, red and yellow enamels, over the glaze. (See chapter on shards of children's plates.)

A small child's mug showing the new unrecorded print The First Nibble also a shard in sepia which had been excavated on the Whitehaven pottery site.

The large fire damaged shard on the right depicts the Beggar's Petition print (the print on the reverse of this small mug depicts the newly recorded print the 'First Nibble').

On examining our children's plate shards I found evidence of *daisy moulded borders,* painted or blobbed, in a variety of vivid colours also *floret borders* (large and small), some dimpled, some filled in, in an octagonal shape, and some in biscuit. A plate showing these characteristics turned up recently (2006) at a B.B.C. 'Antiques Roadshow' at Lancaster. Details were forwarded to me by the owner, the illustration of this print can be seen No. 71 on page 33 of Noel Riley's book 'Gifts for Good Children.' This child's plate has a Whitehaven factory moulded border showing the rose, tulip and aster (plain, not overpainted) and the *impressed star mark on the reverse*.

However in 1998 a Lord of the realm sent me a photograph of his Nursery plate depicting the Whitehaven Print *The Train* which I'm certain was made for Queen Victoria's Coronation in 1838 or for her wedding in 1840, this shows the same shape and characteristics as our shards i.e. the florets are blobbed with red and blue whilst the inner row has been left white, it also has the impressed star on it's reverse, therefore made at the Whitehaven factory.

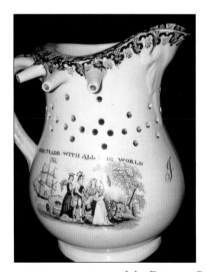 

John Ferguson Puzzle Jug – a late entry.

WHITEHAVEN POTTERY CHILDREN'S PLATES

OBJECT	PRINT	WHOLE POT	ORIGIN	DESCRIPTION	DATE OF POT
1. Child's plate	THE ROMP – identical to Noel Riley's print page 49 Item 142 however Riley shows the Alphabet border. I have not found any pots or shards with this border.	Whole pot	NEC Fair at Birmingham. author's collection.	Creamware, underglaze printed in pale black/white. Border nearly the same as the Young Charioteer in Noel Riley's book 'Gifts for Good Children' Page 196, item 748 i.e. sprigs of blue with green foliage.	1820-40
2. Child's plate	KEEPING SCHOOL – print illustrated by Noel Riley is recorded as a reverse print to our earlier Whitehaven pottery print.	Whole pot	NEC Fair 2004 Birmingham, author's collection.	Creamware, underglaze printed in pale black/white. Border nearly the same as N.Riley's book 'Gifts for Good Children' page 196 items 748 i.e. Sprigs of foliage with red flowers.	1820-40
3. Child's plate	NOW I'M GRANDMOTHER	Whole pot	NEC Fair, 2004 Birmingham. Author's collection.	Creamware, printed in black/white. Border identical to the one Illustrated in Noel Riley's book page 196, item 748 also the Keeping School plate.	1820-40

WHITEHAVEN POTTERY CHILDREN'S PLATES – *Continued*

OBJECT	PRINT	WHOLE POT	ORIGIN	DESCRIPTION	DATE OF POT
4. Child's plate	BEGGAR'S PETITION	Whole pot and a shard fire damaged.	NEC Fair at Birmingham. Author's collection.	Earthenware, underglaze printed in black/white with a black painted line around the rim. Moulded hanging garlands of flowers surrounding the outer rim. Identical to that illustrated in N. Riley's book page 203, item 775.	1820-40.
5. Child's plate	LITTLE TITTY	Whole pot	NEC Fair at Birmingham 2005 Author's collection.	Creamware, underglaze printed in a palette of green, this print is on our darning eggs. It has a moulded border. There is also a nursery plate recorded with fish scale border see page 119.	1820-40.

WHITEHAVEN POTTERY, SHARDS OF CHILDREN'S PLATES.

The Revd., John Fletcher in blue/white has now been recorded. A great many shards were excavated on the factory site which were recorded by the author in the N.C.S. Newsletter No. 115, September, 1999, page 21.

Excavated shards and a whole plate bought at theJan., 2008 Fine Art Fair at the N.E.C. Birmingham. Shards from the Whitehaven Pottery site of the Revd, John Fletcher on children's nursery plates.

According to the Revd., Roger Lee, B.A. in his book *A Short Guide to Wesleyania and Methodist Pottery,* page 3, he claims only a sprinkling of items exist depicting the Revd., John Fletcher.

Whilst attending the N.E.C. Antiques Fair at Birmingham in 2004 I noticed that the Revd., John Wesley small children's plates were selling for approximately £1,000.

*September 1749 the Revd., John Wesley made the first of 26 visits to Whitehaven and founded the first Society of Methodists in the County. The first Chapel was formally registered for Methodist worship in 1761.

In the book on the *History of Cumbria Methodism* by John Burgess, Association and Reform Issues, it states on page 59 that in 1835 there was a County Methodist Membership of 5,000.

The following is an extract from correspondence with the author from Professor Frank Wayling, Professor of the study of Religion at Edinburgh University.**

---

* *Courtesy of Miss Anne Dick, Local Studies Librarian at the Daniel Hay Library, Whitehaven, who pointed me in the direction of research by Sheila Smith, September, 1997, The Methodist Churches and Society of West Cumbria 1761-1997.*

** *Courtesy of Mrs Joyce Chitty, Hest Bank, Mr Roger Edmundson, Shropshire and Rev. Maurice Wright, Vicar of Wem. Shropshire who also informed me that the John Wesley records are kept in The John Rylands Library, Manchester.*

'The Revd., John Fletcher was a great friend of John Wesley. When Wesley was ill in the 1770s, Fletcher was designated to succeed him as leader but Fletcher died in the early 1780s whilst Wesley lived on.

In appearance Fletcher looked somewhat like Wesley so your plates could be either. The date of London, March, 1791 is adventitious. It is after Fletcher had died, but that is not important in that Fletcher was a very significant early Methodist (even though he was an Anglican Vicar) and it is eminently possible that pottery plates etc., were made of him.

He was above all famous for his saintliness. Voltaire who lived in Switzerland where Fletcher (Jean Guillaume de la Flachère) came from, mentioned him as one whose life lived up to the model set by Christ in the Gospels. Fletcher also wrote for Wesley at the time of the Calvinist Controversy in the 1770s in his Arminian writings against Antinomanism which they accused Calvinists of abetting. His fame as a saint lived on, his early fame as a writer faded. John Wesley's own brief life of Fletcher after his death is taken from Rev. Prof. Frank Waylings volume in '*The Classics of Western Spirituality*', volume on John and Charles Wesley which is sold in Britain by S.P.C.K. This tribute records Fletcher's wife to be the source of his information on this very private man.'

Two small christening or birthday plate shards, the lettering on a tablet, these would be given as presents, cheap and cheerful.

To date I have not recorded a whole example of these small black printed and inscribed christening or birthday plates. The larger of the two shards has a shamrock moulded border and the part lettering A Pres.......whilst underneath my Dear. The small shard is also black printed and depicts a gothic style printed border around the inner rim, whilst the centre wording is surrounded by hexagonal double lines. The

A Royal Favourite Child's plate.

A large shard from the Whitehaven site which depicts the Royal Favourite print which is identical to the plate illustrated on the left.

These shards are the first time this print has been recorded, it is The First Nibble *which I discovered quite by accident, as it was the reverse print depicted on a small child's mug which showed the* Beggars Petition *print on the front. The discovery of the larger of the two shards, I have recorded previously in the N.C.S Qtrly Newsletter.*

letter A…(a capital letter) can be seen and below it the part printed letter fo….

In the *Antiques Dealer and Collector's Magazine,* Dec., 1998 Page 31 Rosalind Pulver wrote an article entitled Collectable Ceramics of the 1840-70 period, in which she illustrated a child's plate *Royal Favourite's.* (7″ in diameter).

N.C.S Newsletter No. 118, Figure 4, Page 22, the author illustrates shards which depict this print together with the same triple daisy moulded border and hand painted rim, overglaze painted in various vivid enamels.

These small plates would probably have been made as commemorative items in celebration of the marriage of H.M. Queen Victoria in 1840.

The Playmates with sponged border, however no pots recorded to date. Possibly another nursery plate.

The Garden Flow.
however no pots recorded to date.

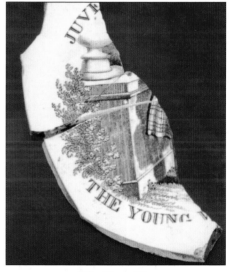

*The Young W…
I'm certain the caption above this print should read 'Juvenile Companions' this plate would be one of a series made at the Whitehaven factory, as our shards prove. Noel Riley illustrates other unmarked plates in this series on page 57 of her book 'Gifts for Good Children' published by Richard Dennis, in 1991.

Jacks Birt...
Noel Riley illustrates a small plate,
unmarked with a moulded border of
roses, thistles and shamrocks, with
the caption above the centre print.
She goes on to say another plate has
been recorded showing this print
with a border of painted sprigs in
red and green. See page 117, where
I illustrate three Whitehaven plates
with this border. It is also on the
'Young Charioteer' *plate, see* Noel
Riley, on page 197 No. 748, also
excavated shards shown below.

Excavated shards of the Young Charioteer and shamrock border.

Young lady seated, the print is Keeping School.

PRINT ON PLATE	COLOUR OF PRINT ON PLATE	BORDER, IF ANY, on SHARD	SOURCE OF PLATE PRINT
1. Part of the word *FAVOURITES* plus part of the print, i.e. puppies in a basket. Should read *Royal Favourite's*.	Black and White underglaze printed	Triple Daisy moulded border. The outer rim of daisies alternating in a red and green paint. No Mark.	See Antique and Collector's Guide Dec., 1998, page 31. An article by Rosalind Pulver *Collecting Later Blue Transfer Printed Pottery. See also N.C.S. Newsletter No. 118 2000 page 22, fig.4*
2. Part words in capitals THE--- AYMATES.	Black and White underglaze printed.	A sponge mixture of blue and red paint covers the border rim. No mark.	Plate not yet identified.
3. Plate shard showing below the print in capitals *THE YOUNG W--*, above the print in capitals *JUVE--* The print shows a garden plinth, shrubs and part of a girl's Kilt.	Sepia (brown) underglaze printed.	Plate centre shards only. No mark.	Noel Riley's book page 57, items 174 and 175. Shows nearly identical prints named *The Young Sargeant and Juvenile Companions*
4. Plate shard showing the bottom half of a small girl sitting in a small wooden chair. *'KEEPING SCHOOL'*	Sepia (very brown) underglaze printed. This shard is *very light in weight – creamware!*	The shard is of a plate centre. At the 2004 N.E.C. fair I found a child's plate showing this print named 'Keeping School' the border is the same as the *Young Charioteer* plate.	This was an important find. Ref. N.R. Page 49, item 40 and her notes page 22' also item 16 and details on page 11 ref. *Reversal of Transfers*.
5. Large shard the caption under the print reads *THE GARDEN FLOW—*in capital letters.	Sepia (brown) under glaze printed.	The shard shows the bottom half of a young girl wearing a long dress. She is sitting in a rustic garden chair.	Not yet identified.
6. Shard fairly small approx., 2″ square.	In sepia and also in blue/white.	A small boy is fishing whilst two young girls watch him. They are resting on a wall.	This print was recently discovered on a small mug which reads the *First Nibble* under the caption.

PRINT ON PLATE	COLOUR OF PRINT ON PLATE	BORDER, IF ANY, on SHARD	SOURCE OF PLATE PRINT
7. A large number of shards, some in biscuit. Over the print, they read *Revd. John Fletcher* whilst underneath the words *Vicar of Madely, Salop.*, etc.	Earthenware and underglaze printed in blue and white.	A triple daisy moulded border surrounds the portait of the Revd. John Fletcher. The daisies are daubed with alternating red, green and blue paint.	Revd. J. Fletcher was being trained to succeed Revd. John Wesley however he predeceased him. See N.C.S. Newsletter 115, Sept., 1999, page 21, with an acknow-ledgement to Professor Frank Wayling, of Edinburgh University.
8. Shards of *CHRISTENING PLATES.*	Black and White underglaze printed.	Moulded shamrocks.	The inscription reads part words *A Present for a Dear Boy* surrounded with laurel leaves then a border rim of moulded shamrocks.
9. *THE BEGGARS PETITION.* A pious poem by Moss.	Badly fired shard in underglaze brown/white, printed.	No border on this shard.	Noel Riley's book Page 203 Item No. 775, Flora and Fauna.
10. ---*ACK'S BIRT*--- shows children dressing a donkey with garlands of flowers.	Two shards under glaze printed in sepia. Also one is printed in Mulberry and another underglaze printed in black and white.	Noel Riley shows a border with a moulding of rose, thistle and shamrock. The Whitehaven Pottery site excavation threw up a biscuit shard.	Noel Riley's book page 197, item 756, Flora and Fauna.
11. *THE YOUNG CHARIOTEER.*	Two shards in sepia, one in Mulberry and one underglaze printed in black and white. The biscuit shard shows foliage and moulded shamrocks on the rim border.	A Sepia shard shows a child driving a cart also part of a girl's dress and the front legs of a large goat which is harnessed and pulling their cart. The black and white shard depicts the cart's wheel and the passenger. The mulberry shard shows the cart's passenger and driver.	Noel Riley's book page 197, item 748.

PRINT ON PLATE	COLOUR OF PRINT ON PLATE	BORDER, IF ANY, on SHARD	SOURCE OF PLATE PRINT
12. A miniature Christening plate.	Underglaze printed in black/white	The shard is broken towards the rim.	A capital letter A shows on a tablet surround (for the wording). One can see the letter 'f' underneath. The outer rim has a gothic design.

WHITEHAVEN POTTERY, DARNING EGGS, THEIR PRINTS, NAMES AND INITIALS

The prints on these earthenware darning eggs whether *bat printed* or *underglaze printed* are always applied to the eggs in a *horizontal position*. 95% of them are named or initialled and most depict children. They are extremely rare items and were made at the Whitehaven factory. Up to date only 20 have been recorded by the author these past two decades. They are family heirlooms therefore bring good prices at local auctions e.g. £500.

Bat printing

The glue content is placed into a stoneware jar or jug. Boiling water is added to dissolve the mixture which is then poured out approximately a quarter of an inch in thickness onto a tray. When cool it looks and feels like a solid jelly and is now ready for the engraver to use in his printing process. Many of the earliest dated pots show a distortion when the transfer printed paper is taken from his flat copper plate and is placed over the surface of bowls or milk jugs, as the paper creases. Whenever his copper plate becomes 'clogged up' as we say in Cumbria, the engraver rubs it down with a solution called Barbados Tar (Stockholm Tar elsewhere in the Potteries). This tar burns off in his kiln leaving it clean, ready to use again. A further application of linseed oil makes the copper plate ready for the next print.

Mr Henry Sandon, in his many lectures, which I attended at the Abbey Hotel, Malvern, Worcestershire, used to say how he loved to go into the engravers' room with all the lovely smells of the various mixes i.e. Linseed Oil, Alum, Lavender, Umber and Turpentine. Today he might be accused of glue sniffing! The enamel paints were made using coloured ground glass, so that they could be used on a creamware body which requires a high temperature.

Bat printing was used on bone china 30-40 years earlier than on earthenware, the reason being the porosity of the earthenware body caused it to soak up all the oils, therefore the print from the paper tissue engraving vanished. However the use of a coating of linseed oil enabled the earthenware object to become watertight. An added bonus was that the oil burnt off in the firing process, leaving the print outline from the engraver's plate, which then allowed the skilled artists to fill it in.

At this period Whitehaven had a fine school of Marine Artists notably Robert Salmon and Joseph Heard. I think it highly probable that some of these artists would have found part-time work at Mr Wilkinson's pottery, filling in maritime seascapes, the rigging of sails etc., to enable them to have some extra cash. The popular Marseillaise print and the scenery on our soft paste jugs is a classic example of what was achieved. The Maritime Museum in Liverpool houses a wonderful painting by Joseph Heard showing 5 Brocklebank ships which were built in Whitehaven, in full sail off the Whitehaven harbour. The Beacon in Whitehaven houses 10 such paintings.

Recorded from The Cumberland News, 26th August, 2005 by Elizabeth Kay, concerning a sale by Bonham's in September, *2005* a picture of The Brig Martha by Joseph Heard was expected to fetch £15,000.

Illustrated below are 13 known Whitehaven Pottery Darning Egg Prints

1. The Newsboy in Sepia

2. A 222 passenger locomotive emerging from a tunnel.

3. The Organ Grinder.

4. Girl Feeding Her Rabbits.

5. Boys with their kite.

6. Girls sharing an umbrella.

7. The Charity pattern.

8. Little Titty.

9. The Pet

131

10. The Romp print, on 3 objects. On the left a small blue/white mug. Centre a small creamware plate with enamelled sprigs, over the glaze, on the border. On the right a darning egg.

11. Now I'm Grandmother.

12. The young nurse.

13. Keeping school.

The following illustrations show darning eggs printed with names or initials.

MARY.ANN F.

WILLIAM K.

MARGARET.JANE

ROBERT

Gift from the Pottery

JAMES. F.

The initials F.G.L.

The initials S.A.S.

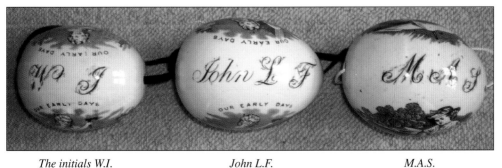

The initials W.I.   *John L.F.*   *M.A.S.*

WHITEHAVEN POTTERY CERAMIC DARNING EGGS, THEIR PRINTS NAMES and INITIALS

NAME OF PRINT	PRINT COLOUR AND DATE	OWNER OF EGG	NAME OR INITIAL ON EGG	SOURCE OF PRINT	INDEX
1. The Newsboy; the print on the reverse shows a train coming through a tunnel.	Sepia (brown). Bat printed 1820-40. A second egg is recorded in black/white.	A local man bought this egg at Messrs. Mitchells Auction Company, Cockermouth. A second egg is owned by a Lord of the Realm.	JAMES F within a cartouche.	According to Noel Riley's book page 167 item 162 the print comes under the heading Occupations and Trades	This print was also used by Edge and Malkin 1871-1903.
2. Train coming out of a tunnel.	Black printed 1820-40	This egg is owned by a Lord of the Realm.		Noel Riley's book page 159 item 574 under the heading Occupations and Trades.	From Mother's Pictorial Alphabet.
3. The Organ Grinder	Bat printed 1820-40 in mulberry. This proves the Whitehaven pottery is experimenting with colours.	Lady who lived in Moor Row, Cumbria. It has now been passed to her daughter in Yorkshire. A second egg is owned by a Lord of the Realm.		Noel Riley's book records page 169 item 627 – Entertainment and the Organ Man.	From Mother's Pictorial Alphabet.
4. A little girl feeding her rabbits. Three eggs have been recorded.	They are all black printed 1820-40.	These are owned by by local men.	MARGARET JANE WILLIAM K & and M.A.S.	Noel Riley records page 215 item 843, under Flora and Fauna.	From Mother's Pictorial Alphabet.
5. Boys flying their kite. A second egg has been recorded in this print.	Both are Black printed 1820-40.	Pearson Collection of St. Bees. A second egg is in the Beacon Collection, Whitehaven.	The Beacon egg has a black/white ribbon threaded through the centre.	Noel Riley recorded this print page 63 item 202 under the Games and Pastimes.	From Mother's Pictorial Alphabet.

WHITEHAVEN POTTERY CERAMIC DARNING EGGS, THEIR PRINTS NAMES and INITIALS

NAME OF PRINT	PRINT COLOUR AND DATE	OWNER OF EGG	NAME OR INITIAL ON EGG	SOURCE OF PRINT	INDEX
6. Two girls sharing an umbrella. Four eggs are recorded with this print.	Two are black printed and two are in sepia with either a red or blue ribbon threaded through the centre.	Pearson Collection Local men Tony Calvin, Cliff Mason also a Carlisle man.	MARGARET. JANE M.A.S. (in black) MARY ANN F. A gift from the Pottery.	Noel Riley records page 50 item 149 under the heading Flora and Fauna.	From Mother's Pictorial Alphabet.
7. Charity, a lady handing bread over a garden wall to two young children.	Black printed 1820-40.	Ike Sloan bequest to the Whitehaven Museum (now the Beacon). A second egg is owned by a local lady Mrs Mary Wilson, Whitehaven.	In script F.G.L.	N.R.'s book page 259 Item 1035 under the heading Piety and Virtue. Noel names this Begging Arms.	From Mother's Pictorial Alphabet.
8. Little Titty. A young girl cradles a black/white pussy	Black printed 1820-40.	The Beacon, Whitehaven. See illustration of this egg on book cover of Volumne I published in 1991.	Norel Riley illustrates a child's plate with a border depicted on Whitehaven pottery children's plates.	N.R.s. book page 207 item 799 under the heading Flora and Fauna.	This Whitehaven pottery egg print is illustrated under the heading Our Early Days.
9. The Pet, the print shows a small girl putting a bonnet on her pet dog. The reverse print is The Romp.	Black printed 1820-40.	Author	In script S.A.S.	N.R.s book The Pet page 49 item 137	From the Mother's Pictorial Alphabet.
10. Now I'm Grandmother.	Black printed 1820-40.	Tony Calvin local man.	W.I. In script.	N.R.s book page 49 item 135	From Mother's Pictorial Alphabet.

WHITEHAVEN POTTERY CERAMIC DARNING EGGS, THEIR PRINTS NAMES and INITIALS – *Continued*

NAME OF PRINT	PRINT COLOUR AND DATE	OWNER OF EGG	NAME OR INITIAL ON EGG	SOURCE OF PRINT	INDEX
11. The Romp.	A little girl is skipping.	Tony Calvin local man.	John L.F.	N.R.s book page 49 item 135.	From Mother's Pictorial Alphabet.
12. The Young Nurse A small girl cradles her pussy which she has wrapped in a blanket.	Black printed 1820-40.	A large darning egg shard has recently been excavated by local man Tony Calvin. The reverse print shows Now I'm Grandmother.		N.R.s book page 207 item 800.	From Mother's Pictorial Alphabet.
13. Keeping School The print on the reverse is that of a girl feeding her rabbits.	In sepia 1820-40.	A Carlisle man.	This egg has a ribbon through the centre.	N.R.s book page 49 items 140.	From Mother's Pictorial Alphabet.

WHITEHAVEN POTTERY, CERAMIC BELL/CURTAIN PULLS 1820-40

In 1996 the then editors of the N.C.S. Newsletter, the late Clarice and her husband Harold Blakey, whilst on a ceramic seminar on the Isle of Wight, visited Osborne House, where they spotted one of the Whitehaven factory's ceramic eggs holding back the heavy drapes surrounding Her Majesty Queen Victoria's bed. They communicated the information to me immediately.

I approached English Heritage requesting a photograph. The Curator (1997) replied telling me that *unfortunately he could not supply a catalogue entry as they only had a basic inventory of the contents*, however he very kindly measured their egg for me. It was like the rest of our curtain/bellpull eggs which had been recorded i.e. 12.5cm or 5″ in length.

Mrs Margaret Crosby, senior reporter for the *Whitehaven News*, wrote an article. Shortly afterwards a local man who had visited Osborne House, and bought the Official Guide, made contact. He offered me his copy of the guide and there it is, in glorious colour, a Whitehaven pottery bell/curtain pull. Unfortunately I cannot reproduce the photograph; however it gives me great pleasure to think that one Easter time the Earl of Lonsdale had presented Her Majesty Queen Victoria with this *Whitehaven pottery curtain/bell pull*.

The Beacon Museum in Whitehaven has two of these rare eggs in their collection of Whitehaven pots. These two eggs depict three different underglaze prints black printed, two to each egg. One is a print of a large Pyrethrum type flower head whilst a second is of stylised flower. The third print shows four Alexander type roses amidst foliage

Ceramic curtain/bell pull depicting pyrethrum type flower.

Stylised flower.

*The third print on these eggs shows four
Alexander type roses amidst foliage.*

*A blue spongeware curtain pull egg in The
Beacon Collection*

A Mr Alan Cornish of Macclesfield owns the egg on the left, a family heirloom. It shows initials, in script, E.J.K. plus a ribbon which has been threaded through the centre of the egg. Alan reckons the initials were those of his grandmother Elizabeth Green, nee Kellett, previously of Whitehaven. As well as these initials the egg depicts the print showing the four individual Alexander type roses amidst acanthus leaves. The photographs are those of Mr Alan Cornish of Macclesfield.

*Mr Alan Cornish's ceramic bell/curtain pull showing initials and the same print as that on the Beacon
egg which shows four Alexander type roses amidst acanthus leaves.*

The author managed to purchase one of these eggs in April, 2004 at Mitchells Auction Rooms, in Cockermouth, Cumbria. This egg depicts three individual prints, one illustrates a stalk of gooseberries, a second a stalk of strawberries whilst the third is a floral print.

The images on these bell pulls are printed vertically whereas the darning eggs are printed horizontally.

A stalk of gooseberries.

A stalk of strawberries.

A floral print.

THE NINETEENTH CENTURY *Continued*
OTHER POTTERIES

THE CARLISLE POTTERY

● CARLISLE POTTERY: On Blackwell Road, later converted to a bone manure works
Picture: Ashley Kendall

The above article appeared in 'The Cumberland News' on the 21st November, 2003 it was written by Denis Perriam and headed 'Past and Present'. The illustration is courtesy of Mr Ashley Kendall.

I have attempted to transcribe part of the article herewith.

'Using the pen-name Solway, Walter Haydon wrote each week in The Cumberland News about all things Cumbrian. In 1950 he wrote; there seems to have been a pottery of some kind in Carlisle at one time. it is curious that its activities do not appear to have been placed on record'.

It is now possible to re-assess the history of this long forgotten Carlisle industry.

One of the problems was that the pottery was referred to as being at St. Nicholas which was not thought to be Currock. What has not been realised is that Currock did not exist in the 1850s, but was known as St. Nicholas Fields. So when the *Carlisle Journal* announced in July 1854, 'another new manufactory has recently been established… the pottery at St. Nicholas which Messrs Wannop and Nanson have commenced', we know that this is the pottery which stood on Blackwell Road and traded under the name Carlisle Pottery.

He goes on to relate that an advert for the Carlisle Pottery appeared in the *Journal* a year later for 'milk bowls, cream pots, dishes and every description of brown earthenware, garden pots, vases and chimney tops'. These were available at the St. Nicholas works and at the proprietors 'Thomas Nanson and Co., Slaters, 16, Finkle

Street'. The article records that they were still trading in 1858, that they ceased trading in 1861 and the building was to be converted to a bone manure works which existed for some 20 years, then briefly became a marine store for a Mr Long. Maps of the area in the 1890s refer to it as 'The Potteries'.

Confirmation that the manure works was the former pottery comes from the use of part of it in the 1880s and early 1890s as the Pottery Mission Hall. There was even a football team known as the 'Pottery Punters'.

Seemingly the *Cumberland News* in 1953 illustrated a recent addition to Carlisle Museum said to have been made at Currock which bears the mark Carlisle Pottery enclosed in an oval. The reporter claims other pieces exist in the county bearing the same stamp.

THE CLAY FLATTS POTTERY (THE MARSH) WORKINGTON 1861.

The Potters here were Jonnie and Thomas Dunbar. Their pots were mostly moulded items embellished with foliage and animals, rabbits, mice etc. The pots usually show a yellow clay body with a manganese glaze. The vases are approximately 7 inches high. The Helena Thompson Museum in Workington houses a collection of Dunbar pottery jugs etc.

The Dunbar brothers came to Workington from Edinburgh originally. They served their apprenticeships under John Docherty at Fox House (The Pot Kiln) Broughton Moor. In Kelly's Directory 1894 John Dunbar is recorded as living at New Yard Road, Clay Flats, Workington.

Shortly after the publication of my first book in 1991, I received a visit from Mr Clive Lowther of Workington. Clive brought a small grotesque milk jug to show me. It had been given to Clive as a boy, by a spinster aunt (his mother's sister) Elizabeth, born in 1868. Clive's grandparents (Teasdales) were publicans in Senhouse Street; Workington, then later they had a haulage business. His grandfather Teasdale was a friend of the Dunbars.

The iron tobacco jar is on the left and the ceramic jar with lid on the right.

In June, 2001 I sent an article to the Editors of the N.C.S Newsletter with reference to the discovery by my husband of an iron replica. N.C.S Report No.122, page 12, shows both these jugs.

The article was noted by Judy Ely, collections officer at the Rotherham Museum, Yorks. Judy emailed me. She stated that their museum has an iron one in its collection. Rotherham Museum data concerning this jar refers to an article *'Chats on English Tobacco Jars by Reg. Myers* who illustrates two more which he reckons are cast in lead.

A local lady had also read my N.C.S article and whilst attending an antiques fair in West Cumbria recognised another iron one and like the first iron jug it is *hatless*. The stall holder had written *'Easter Island'*, on the underside of her jug, she thought it resembled the statues on Easter Island! The person giggled to herself and thought 'there is no iron on Easter Island, it is in the Pacific', so she bought the jug.

Clive's earthenware milk jug is the only ceramic jug recorded up to now. I am certain that Clive's jug which is wearing a hat and has a hole at the end of it's nose is a milk jug, whilst the three iron ones which are hatless are ashtrays and the two cast in lead, and each wearing a different model of hat, to Clive's, are tobacco jars for holding loose tobacco leaf.

Towards the end of 2004 one of the antiques experts on BBC TV. stated 'these jugs were a satirical caricature of the 19th century comedian Ally Sloper', who resembled yesterday's 'Jimmy Snozzle Durante' with his large nose.

Below is a map showing the whereabouts of the Pottery on Clay Flatts.Workington. (12)

A typical moulded Dunbar jug.

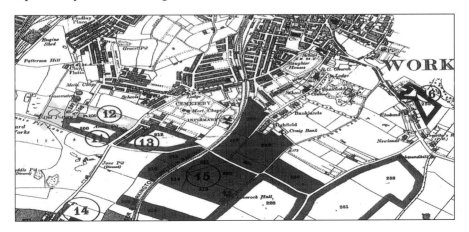

143

CLIFTON (CROSSBARROW) POTTERY, NEAR WORKINGTON.

The following details were taken from the Lowther papers C.R.O. Carlisle. These details prompted my visit to the Crossbarrow Pottery site in April, 1989. A visit which resulted in my finding the large Clifton (inscribed) slipware marriage dish.

Details:-

> 12th October, 1787 received of Henry Scrugham what he received of Henry Fearon for liberty of getting potters clay on the commons in the Manors of Great and Little Clifton, due Christmas 1787,   19s.

> 1788 received of Jeremiah James Potter, Midsummer last   £1.

THE FEARONS

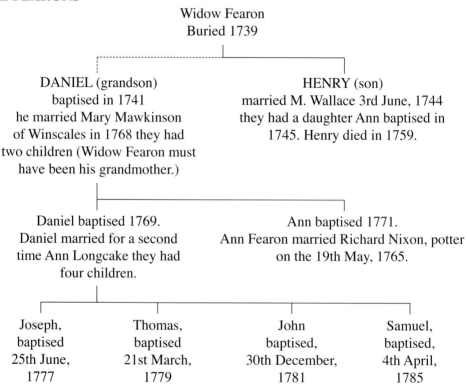

Widow Fearon
Buried 1739

DANIEL (grandson)
baptised in 1741
he married Mary Mawkinson
of Winscales in 1768 they had
two children (Widow Fearon must
have been his grandmother.)

HENRY (son)
married M. Wallace 3rd June, 1744
they had a daughter Ann baptised in
1745. Henry died in 1759.

Daniel baptised 1769.
Daniel married for a second
time Ann Longcake they had
four children.

Ann baptised 1771.
Ann Fearon married Richard Nixon, potter
on the 19th May, 1765.

Joseph,
baptised
25th June,
1777

Thomas,
baptised
21st March,
1779

John
baptised,
30th December,
1781

Samuel,
baptised,
4th April,
1785

The Lowther documents dated 1787 relate to a Henry Fearon paying rent for *potters clay* Christmas, 1787 = 19s. However the same source records, 1788 a Jerimiah James, Potter is paying rent i.e. £1 *for permission for clay.*

JEREMIAH JAMES

1781 He is recorded as working at the Ginns House, Pottery, Whitehaven according to the St. Bees Church registers (*see D. Hay, An Illustrated History of Whitehaven.*)

1781 Jerimiah James married Ann.

their family

Richard buried 1787	1787 Twins Baptised John William	Isobella buried 1788 Jane	Barbara baptised 1790	Ann baptised 1792	Jerimiah William baptised 1794 buried 1797

1789 31st January Jerimiah James is now living and working at Clifton and paying £1 rent for permission to extract clay for potters ware, according to the Lowther documents C.R.O. Carlisle.

These names and dates need a lot of further investigation perhaps by the Clifton Local History Society?

1799 According to the Lowther records *Widow James* paid rental of £1 for permission to dig for clay for pottery ware on the 9th July of this year, so seemingly Jerimiah had died. He had been working the Clifton pottery for 10 years. The Lowther records then show the Blackburn family taking control so we must assume Widow James had sold out.

THE BLACKBURNS

The following names and dates, refering to this Blackburn family of potters, were obtained from the large imposing family headstone which stands in Bridgefoot Church graveyard within the church grounds. The dates marked with an asterick were very kindly given to me by Mr Peter Ostle, Carlisle.

1770 A John Blackburn was baptised.

1796 A Joseph Blackburn married Ann Ostle Her family were potters at nearby Dearham throughout the 19th century. 3rd June, 1815, page 145, Workington Church registers, 1676-1812*

1796 A John Blackburn married Mary Cameron at Little Clifton on the 19th October.

Their three children are as follows.
1798 William Blackburn baptised.*
1810 Thomas baptised.*
1822 Robert baptised.*

---

* *Dates given by Peter Ostle.*

The following list of names is recorded on the family headstone.

1800 John Blackburn was baptised.

1804 John Blackburn aged 4yrs old was buried.

1807 John son of John and Mary was baptised.

1814 Edward baptised, he died 26th February, 1884 aged 70yrs old.*

1817 James was baptised. (he died 11th March, aged 68yrs old)*

1819 George was baptised, son of John and Mary. He died 6th February, 1864 aged 45yrs old.

A Thomas Wallace is recorded on the family tombstone. He was born 1839, and died 4th November, 1914 aged 75 years. Mary his wife died 27th May, 1920 aged 78yrs old.* I have recorded a Wallace in the afore mentioned Fearon family records courtesy of the C.R.O. Carlisle i.e. Henry Fearon married a Mary Wallace on the 3rd June, 1744 so we must presume that these two families had kept in close contact with each other throughout a great number of years. I have also recorded a J. R. Wallace owner of the Distington Private Museum.

The following extract is a local Newspaper account of a funeral at Clifton in 1897. (Courtesy of the Curator of the Helena Thompson Museum, Workington).

Yesterday, Thursday afternoon a large concourse of relatives and friends followed to their last meeting place the remains of Mr William Blackburn a member of the well known Blackburn family who have been connected with the Crossbarrow Pottery at Clifton for a large number of years, his five elders being the owners.

THE CLIFTON SLIPWARE, INSCRIBED AND INITIALLED MARRIAGE DISH

I had discovered an old ordnance survey map of the area in the C.R.O. Carlisle, so decided to walk the area looking for any sign of a clay pit etc. Three *Last of the Summer Wine* type gentlemen assured me, *I was on the right track,* as we say in Cumbria.

Whilst on this site visit, curious owners of a nearby white cottage which bore the date 1666 above the door (now completely unrecognisable due to part demolition and a great deal of money having been spent on renovations and extensions) came to enquire what I was doing. They recognised me! I readily explained and showed them my map. To my amazement one of the two ladies went into the rear of their cottage and brought forth a large slip decorated dish incised into the clay on the reverse Clifton Dish and bearing the initials of the maker I.T. on the front within the Royal Arms. These initials are those of James Tunstall, a local potter. The large dish was a marriage token inscribed to two local folks Edward Harrington and Mary Thompson. James Tunstall's mother went to live with her son Aaron at Crossbarrow according to her death certificate. The Tunstall brothers must have found Stephen Shaw's mould and made a copy. We must presume Stephen Shaw had also made the large dish in the Fitzwilliam Museum before leaving Cumberland but left his mould behind.

---

*   *Dates given by Peter Ostle.*

Six weeks later the well known expert on pottery and porcelain, author, broadcaster and international lecturer Henry Sandon who was staying as a guest whilst giving a series of lectures on behalf of the appeal fund for Carlisle cathedral roof, confirmed it was indeed an 18th century slipware marriage dish.

Arrangements were made to try to get a grant before it was sold. This we did and thanks to grants from the National Art Collection Fund, the Victoria and Albert Museum and the people of Workington and Friends of Workington Museum this very important dish was purchased and can now be seen in the Helena Thompson Museum, Workington. See Chapter 1 for photographs and details of these three dishes.

We excavated the site later, hoping to find a mould but all we discovered was a small eighteenth century slipware cup. The Helena Thompson Museum purchased it from the owner Jim Wilson. It is now displayed in the Museum.

Shard of a handle and a large cider or oil jar.

The eighteenth century slipware cup

The Sandon's and The Chitty's sorting shards from The Clifton Pottery site.

Dining alfresco after digging and sorting shards.

This small cat was excavated on the site by owner Mr Jim Wilson

REBTON HALL (now Ribton) CAMERTON.
HARKER MARSH (WHISTLING SYKE) AND DEARHAM MILL POTTERIES

Aaron Wedgwood the Staffordshire potter was invited to try to make red/creamware at Aikbank, Whitehaven in 1698 however the enterprise failed.

Aaron did not return to Staffordshire but married a local woman Margaret Tunstall, in St. James Church, Whitehaven. They left the Copeland area and went to work at Rebton Hall (now Ribton) near Cockermouth. Perhaps they had joined the Tunstall family of potters!

In 1704 they went to start up on their own, making pottery at Whistling Syke, Harker Marsh, Broughton Moor. No pots survive from this area as it was bulldozed into the ground by British Opencast Coal Company in the 1970s.

A lease in the Lowther Records Carlisle CRO (courtesy of the Lowther Trustees) dated 1731-1746 shows their son's Aaron II & Thomas rented Dearham Mill & Tythes. The lease reads they had to 'keep the mill, kiln & utensils in as good a state as when they enter' See Volume I page 11.

Another document (from the same source) records the family paying for permission to obtain clay on Lord Wharton's land.

According to these same records in 1754 Aaron III (his grandson)had been given permission to extract clay from 4 commons surrounding Whitehaven for 21 years. (the norm for any Lowther estate) See Volume I page 15.

DEARHAM VILLAGE POTTERY

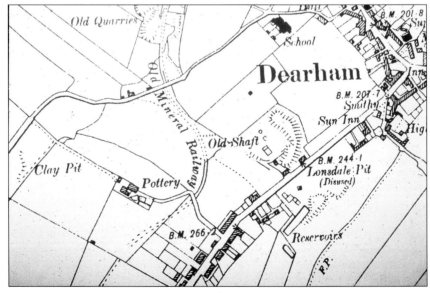

Site of Dearham Pottery

Aaron II started the Dearham Village pottery. He was joined by his son in 1772; Aaron III had been working for Peter How at St. Bees however when Peter How failed financially he had no option but to join his father at the Dearham pottery.

This coarse earthenware pottery was run by the Ostle family from 1817-1883 (note family tree later in this chapter).

This Dearham pottery site was originally excavated by Mr. David Graham in 1996 helped by members of the village Local History Society. Their shards are housed in the Maryport Roman Museum.

They excavated shards of bed pans, brown mugs, slip decorated items, showing a series of dots and only half glazed on the outside etc., etc.

A water container for pigeons or poultry.

Large ashtray.

The surviving whole pots are housed in the Helena Thompson Museum in Workington and are a good example of what the pottery produced; in the main large pots for domestic use. Shaving mugs seem to have been a good selling point and today are family heirlooms. Three have been recorded to date. They fetch good money at auction.

The 1861 Census returns for Dearham, record Mr Wilson Ostle, coarse earthenware

A pig trough made by Wilson Ostle, it shows a pig hanging from the lug handle on the end of the trough.

manufacturer. In 1871 he employed Richard Davis, James Lynch, John Hetherington & John Rutherford as potters whilst Ann Davis is described as a pottery labourer & 14 years old Robinson Harrison a boy apprentice, whilst John McKenzie describes himself as a retired potter. The 1883 Bulmer's Directory for West Cumberland records Wilson Ostle still managing this pottery.

Bulb pots were a popular item. One has been passed down through the Wedgwood family. Please note the similarity of decoration with these and the Isaac Moore tobacco jar (illustrated

Tobacco jar made for Mariner Isaac Moore, of St. Bees. I think the owner, now deceased, thought this had been made at the Ginns House pottery (the earliest known Whitehaven pottery). I'm now convinced these were all made by Aaron Wedgwood III at the Dearham pottery.

Note the similarity of decoration between the Isaac Moore tobacco jar above and the bulb pot. Also the E.W. inscribed & decorated bulb pot illustrated below. Do we also have the same family association i.e. the Clifton Marriage Dish and the Harrington family, as the initials are E.H.M. & P.H.N on the bulb pot? The photographs of the P.H.N. inscribed bulb pot are courtesy of Mr Tom Walford, Editor of 'The Transactions' of the English Ceramic Circle.

The Wedgwood family bulb pot, a family heirloom.

The reverse, this compares with the Isaac Moore Tobacco Jar.

This pot is owned by a Workington Town Councillor.

below) which has the same date 1791 (incidentally the date Revd John Wesley died).

The Wedgwood family heirloom inscribed E.W. and dated 1810, is said to have been made for Aaron Wedgwood's 70th birthday. The local potter has made the mistake of putting an 'E' instead of an 'A' I gather a common occurrence in the family. (I blame the pronunciation on the Cumbria dialect.). Courtesy of the wife of the late Mr Tom Mitchell, *ex Manager of the Great Britain Rugby League Team*. She was a 'Cumbrian Wedgwood'. The pot belongs to her brother.

A Dearham pottery shaving bowl, formerly the property of William Dobinson born 15th April, 1861, bought by him from Anthony Bigney who worked at Dearham pottery during the 19th century was sold at Penrith Kydd and Farmers Auctions, Penrith in 2003, it fetched £380 plus VAT etc.

A family heirloom, a second Dearham pottery coarse earthenware shaving mug, dated and initialled.

A selection of domestic pots, slip decorated and dated. These were much frowned upon until the Lakeland poet John Ruskin declared 'They are as nature'.

Kelly's Directory 1894 records a 'Scott Williams' as being in business at Main Street, Cockermouth as a 'China Riveter'. *Items of pottery displaying metal rivets are collector's items these days.*

JON VOYEZ

In June, 1996, I purchased, second hand, a copy of Guide No. 1, The Delholm Gallery, of the contents of the Mint Museum, Carolina, U.S.A. On page 22 a small moulded earthenware teapot (dated 1770) was attributed to John Voyez, (said to be French) a modeller for the great Josiah Wedgwood of Staffordshire, England.

According to Josiah's biographer Eliza Meteyard, this man proved to be a scoundrel. In fact Josiah Wedgwood had the man jailed. Later when *Voyez was released, Josiah wrote to his friend Bentley claiming Voyez was undercutting him with his basalt seals and he thought Voyez had stolen moulds from his factory!*

A document in the archives of the Beacon Museum & Art Gallery, Whitehaven concerning Peter How records French ships in the harbour and 'five more coming' (Jon Voyez was French!)

During the 2nd Jacobite Rebellion of 1745-6 a French prisoner named John Boyer had his sentence of death *reprieved* at Carlisle Jail. Instead, he was sent to the 'House of Correction' in Whitehaven, but never arrived! I record a copy of this document later.

I wish to quote from Mr Michael Finlay's book '*Western Writing Implements*' published by Plains Books, 1990 'in the secretary hand there is little difference between the z & r'. The Head Jailer at Carlisle (possibly not an educated man) could easily have written 'John Boyer' instead of 'Jon Voyez'. He would then present his book for signature, to Sir Everard Falconer, secretary to the Duke of Cumberland.

The prisoners were later marched to the jail at Whitehaven (known as the House of Correction), the date 1745. An expenses claim, submitted to Sir Everard Falconer by the head jailer at *Whitehaven*, for subsistence, named the prisoners. *John Boyer's name was not included on the list.* (see following page).

45 - The following document records a Joseph Wild, Sergeant of the Whitehaven Volunteers requesting payment for marching the Dukes' prisoners from Blackhall, Carlisle to Whitehaven together with a copy of the list of prisoners sent to the Keeper of the Whitehaven Jail and schedule of expenses. Once again there is no *John Boyer* listed.

Did John Boyer (alias Jon Voyez) come to Whitehaven to work as modeller for Wedgwood III and later Peter How at St. Bees. Then, when the amnesty was declared between Britain & France in 1748, board a ship in Whitehaven to London where he became acquainted with the great Josiah? Possibly informing Josiah he had been working for his Cumbrian cousins.

D/HUD/18/9. The 1745 'The Aftermath'. (Courtesy of C.R.O. Whitehaven.)
This is a copy of the document referring to the prisoners captured in the Jacobite rebellion at Carlisle, Cumberland, courtesy of Miss Susan Dench, a Senior Archivist, C.R.O. Carlisle.

A List of the Charge of Maintaining the Prisoners in the House of Correction at Whitehaven at 12 [d] [per] Week Since Jul[y] 16th [17...]

N°.	Persons Names	Dead or Escaped	Crime	Time wks	Charge £ s d
1	Valentine Clark	—	On Suspicion of Felony	12 0 0	— 12 —
2	Andrew Rumney	Escaped	For Felony	3 6	— 3 —
4	Samuel Clark	Escaped	For Felony & High Treason	3 6	— 3 —
5	W[m] Lockey	—	For High Treason	12 0 0	— 12 —
6	W[m] Donkin	—	For D°	12 0 0	— 12 —
7	John Campble	—	For D°	12 0 0	— 12 —
	John Wallace	—	For D°	12 0 0	— 12 —
	Tho[s] Lawson	—	For D°	12 0 0	— 12 —
	Joseph Mead	—	For D° Suspicion	12 0 0	— 12 —
	Alex[r] Leslie	—	For D°	12 0 0	— 12 —
	Joseph Parrot	—	For D° Suspicion	12 0 0	— 12 —
	Peter Garn alias Gardiner	—	For D°	12 0 0	— 12 —
	Angus Grant alias M[c]Lennan	Removed to London	For D°	9 0 0	— 9 —
	Jonathan Cristman	—	For D° Suspicion	12 0 0	— 12 —
	Ralph Price	—	For D°	12 0 0	— 12 —
	W[m] Wenslowley	—	For D°	12 0 0	— 12 —
	George Hartley	—	For D°	12 0 0	— 12 —
	Robert Davie	—	For D°	12 0 0	— 12 —
	Thomas Hatch	—	For D°	12 0 0	— 12 —
	W[m] Stuart	—	For D°	12 0 0	— 12 —
	John M[c]Intosh	—	For D°	12 0 0	— 12 —
	Dugal Campble	—	For D°	12 0 0	— 12 —
	Eley Jollenson	—	For D°	12 0 0	— 12 —
	Ann Layread	—	For D°	12 0 0	— 12 —
	Jane Mathewson	—	For D°	12 0 0	— 12 —
	Marg[t] Stranghson	—	For D°	12 0 0	— 12 —
	W[m] Bryan	—	For D° Suspicion	12 0 0	— 12 —
	Christopher Hornsby	—	For Suspicion after proclamation	12 0 0	— 12 —
	John Thompson	—	For High Treason	12 0 0	— 12 —
	Rob[t] Muckle	—	D° Suspicion	12 0 0	— 12 —
					16 19 0
	For Straw for them to lye in	—	post paid		8

Quarter sessions 1746, Easter petitions-30 Q11-132.

Account for the period, records prisoner's names, (dead or escaped), crime, period in custody, and cost of keep. All but 3 felons are there for High Treason and were Jacobites (several Scots amongst them). Carlisle Petty Sessions recorded 21 men guarded these prisoners at Carlisle for one month at 1s per day per man.

1747 Easter-both France & the English had prisoners of war. Midsummer, a warrant was issued for three to be released on both sides. It is possible that this was when Jon Voyez, known locally as John Boyer, obtained his freedom.

1748 France & Britain concluded the *'Treaty of Aix la Chappelle'* when France pledged not to permit any member of the Stuart family to reside in France.

'A House of Correction'.

The following relates to the distinction between a jail & a house of correction. A jail is a prison for the accommodation of those convicted on suspicion of a felony or misdemeanour. A House of Correction was a place maintained by the County for the keeping and correcting and setting to work of rogues, vagabonds and sturdy beggars . . . Was *Jon Voyez* alias *John Boyer* such a prisoner?

When Jon Voyez (alias John Boyer) was released from prison in Staffordshire, his knowledge concerning the pottery trade in Whitehaven meant he could easily make connections in order to sell his moulds and wares.

An advertisement by a *Tinsmith in Whitehaven Market Place*, records the tinsmith trading in *black basalt seals*. The advertisement stated he was acting as agent to the Staffordshire potter Sam Greenwood who could neither read nor write. A man who had signed the marriage register with an 'X,' yet the experts have recorded a vase said to have been signed by him. *'Western Writing Implements'* Page 185 illustrates a 'fob seal' described in dark red stoneware which he claims is impressed *VOYEZ* whom he describes as 'an émigré potter who worked for Josiah Wedgwood & Ralph Wood before starting up on his own'.

The following is an advertisement in the *Cumberland Pacquet* 11/8/1778

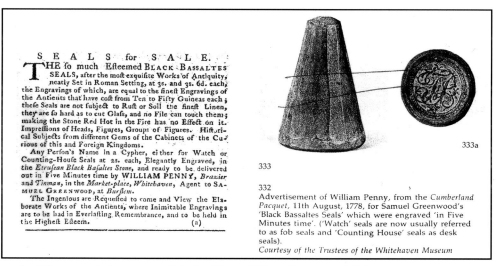

SEALS for SALE.

THE so much Esteemed BLACK BASSALTES SEALS, after the most exquisite Works of Antiquity, neatly Set in Roman Setting, at 3s. and 3s. 6d. each, the Engravings of which, are equal to the finest Engravings of the Antients that have cost from Ten to Fifty Guineas each ; these Seals are not subject to Rust or Soil the finest Linen, they are so hard as to cut Glass, and no File can touch them ; making the Stone Red Hot in the Fire has no Effect on it. Impressions of Heads, Figures, Groups of Figures. Historical Subjects from different Gems of the Cabinets of the Curious of this and Foreign Kingdoms.

Any Person's Name in a Cypher, either for Watch or Counting-House Seals at 2s. each, Elegantly Engraved, in the *Etrufean Black Bafaltes Stone*, and ready to be delivered out in Five Minutes time by WILLIAM PENNY, *Brazier* and *Tinman*, in the *Market-place, Whitehaven*, Agent to SAMUEL GREENWOOD, at *Burslem*.

The Ingenious are Requested to come and View the Elaborate Works of the Antients, where Inimitable Engravings are to be had in Everlasting Remembrance, and to be held in the Highest Esteem.   (a)

333a

333

332

Advertisement of William Penny, from the *Cumberland Pacquet*, 11th August, 1778, for Samuel Greenwood's 'Black Bassaltes Seals' which were engraved 'in Five Minutes time'. ('Watch' seals are now usually referred to as fob seals and 'Counting House' seals as desk seals).
Courtesy of the Trustees of the Whitehaven Museum

I wish to quote from an article by Diana Edwards, ceramic historian.
'Black Basalt, Wedgwood & Contemporary Manufacture' referring to Sam Greenwood, (the man I suspect is now working for Jon Voyez and sending black basalt seals to Whitehaven). Diana Edwards says 'Nothing is known of this manufacture. Jewett indicates that a potter named Greenwood was operating in Fenton from about 1770/80 but gives no information. Were it not for the existence of a black basalt vase in the British Museum the Greenwood name would be relegated to oblivion. The very handsome vase is not unlike those produced by Wedgwood & Bentley, and Palmer & Neale, if a bit heavier and slightly more awkward in execution. Grant feels the one distinguishing feature in the Greenwood vase is the band of oak leaves at the shoulder'.

Yet again just like the small inscribed creamware teapots mentioned in an earlier chapter, is this John Voyez sending Josiah Wedgwood's moulds and black basalt seals to the Wedgwoods of Cumberland?

I have good reason to make these facts known as we have in West Cumberland a great many of these small teapots which show the identical moulding to the Mint Museum teapot which experts have attributed to Jon Voyez.

Jean Sanders, a local historian, (speciality subject local wills) recently showed me the Will of Jane Mulcaster. At the time of her will Margaret Jane Mulcaster made Phillip Wedgwood b.1876 and a Joseph Wallace Mulcaster, Mining Engineer of St. Bees, executors of her will. On page 147, I illustrate and record Kenneth Mulcaster's small teapot which is identical to the Mint Museum teapot.

Kenneth Mulcaster's small moulded teapot.   *This one was sold by Mitchells Auction Co., Ltd. in the 1990s.*

We have recorded a number of these small teapots in West Cumberland in recent years. According to the *Workington Times & Star*, 29th August, 1957 a Dr Frank Alpin, Director of Medicine, Fort Worth, Texas, U.S.A. owned one of these small moulded teapots and declared it had been brought out to the U.S.A. by his family who had previously lived in West Cumbria.

The Ostle family of potters at Dearham.

Following is the family tree of the Ostle family of potters recorded and sent to me by a member of the Cumberland Family History Society Mr Peter Ostle. We made contact when Peter was recording the folks connected with the village of Holm Cultram, near Carlisle. I was able to tell Peter that the Sibson family were Church Wardens at the Abbey Church a number of centuries ago!

It is with sadness that I *now record the destruction of this fine abbey of 'Holm Cultram' which was destroyed by fire in June, 2006.*

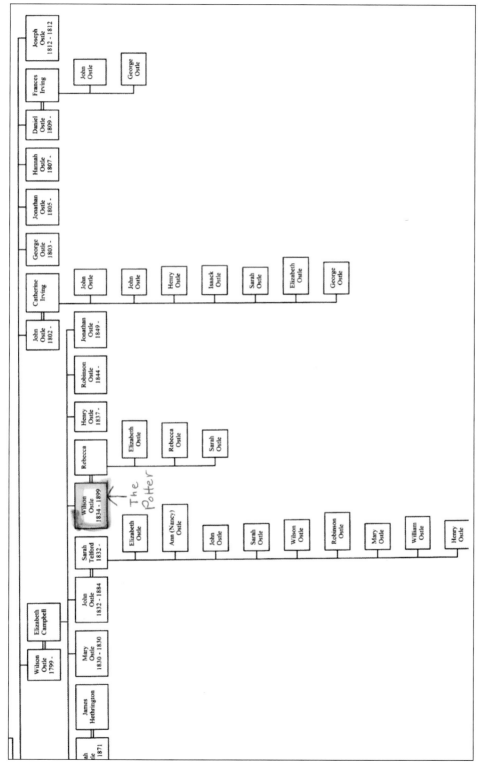

Sheet 1 showing Wilson Ostle the Dearham potter.

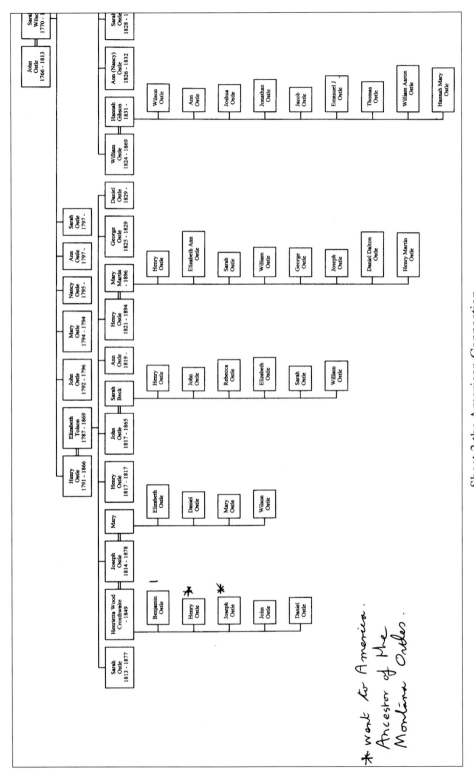

Sheet 2 the American Connection
Peter shows the Ostle family connection as far as Montana, U.S.A.

* went to America.
Ancestor of the
Montana Ostles.

Dearham Village Pottery (location Pottery Lane off Wedgwood Crescent) Dearham

The archaeological excavations were started *16th October, 2006* by the North Pennines Archaeological Unit who are based at Carlisle.

Team, Matthew Town, Jo (female), Joe Doran Frank Chico, Catherine Peters (leader) (not in attendance when we visited on *Wednesday, 18th October, 2006)*.

The site had started to be excavated. A lottery grant had been obtained by Dearham Parish Council. The two logos on Joyce Percival's newsheet to the villagers of Dearham are the *Big Lottery Fund* and the other is the *Cumbria Community Foundation*. It was *'Awards for All'* and the *'Allerdale Invest'*.

Site visit – *Monday, 23rd October, 2006*. In attendance Matt Town and Kevin (a new member), told me on the previous Friday they had excavated spindle wheels, as used by village ladies for weaving. I had not seen any of those before. Joyce Percival showed me two wasters which looked like miners tokens (in a red clay) with a thumb print on. The experts on Channel 4s *Time Team* on 6th March, 2008, discovered similar objects in Cornwall and explained what they were. This was interesting as Ester Saul whose name is inscribed on a creamware teapot I have recorded had married Jonathan Harris of the Harris Weaving Mill in Cockermouth. This company had royal patronage at that time, not only did they supply woven cloth but their team of Embroiders supplied garments made to order for H.M. Queen Victoria. I remembered the late Clarice Blakey (co-editor of the N.C.S. Newsletter), wrote an article on Knitting Sheaths and recorded a sheath owned by Ester Saul. These held the knitting needles in place once the ends are tucked underneath a lady' arms.

Later that morning Kevin excavated part of either a bowl or chamber pot in flow blue (which the Americans love) with a flat rim depicting small violets under the glaze. (Flow blue was obtained by accident, when ammonia was thrown into a kiln and the cobalt ran!) Perhaps a kiln man was caught short and used the inside of his kiln (ammonia)!

Jo was excavating the trench (bottom right, the clay plunging pond) where she unearthed a small bottle and a clay pipe with the initials T.W. (Thomas Wood) the initials of the main mould maker of Leith, Scotland. I uncovered shards of chicken feeders.

Wed, 25th October, 2006

In charge Jo, also there were Dana from Canada, Joe (male) the trench digger, and Alan, a volunteer digger, who mentioned he was researching the large, now disused, textile mill in Carlisle.

Donald and I were put to work cleaning the moss and grass off the impressive building Dana had discovered, thought to be a drying house for pots. The floor of this building was laid out in bricks, many impressed Dearham Colliery and Wilson, Broughton Moor. The walls, running in parallel, consisted of large cut quarried stones from nearby. However, depending on their size, they were sometimes two deep, with a gap between which was filled with broken pieces of sagger. The three large slate slabs at the entrance were approximately 2-3 ft. square.

Photos of the Dearham excavations

Location of site.

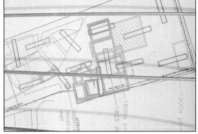

The trenches.

Author digging

The ink well

Unglazed base of ink well.

Bank of shards.

A chicken feeder.

Joyce and Matthew Town.

1865 1st edition O.S. Map showing the Dearham pottery site.

Clay pipe showing T.W.

Alan excavating.

Spindle wheel

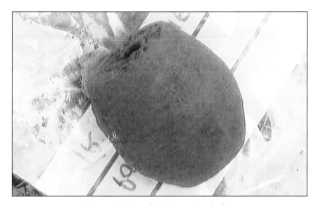

Barrel shaped with centre hole.

Donald started working on a building behind Dana's which showed more wear and tear. The entrance consisted of another large slate slab. Joe was busy excavating the trench which resembled a clay pit. Jo as well as supervising us all, was busy excavating the clay ponds, whilst Alan excavated the building next to the field. A second building which had a single brick wall had identical brick floors which were also laid down on their sides.

What did we discover:-
A large piece of flint approx. 4 inches in size.
Two large shards of slipware.
Various domestic bowls, their rims showing one, two or three circles of slip onto their manganese glazed body.

Jo allowed me to photograph the weaving spindles which Joyce had uncovered.

Alan showed me a ball of white ball clay, the size of a golf ball, and enquired what I thought

Trench top rt. showing large bowl shards.

it might be. I realised it was a ball of pipe clay ready for the potter to push into his pipe mould. One that had gone astray hence our lucky discovery.

Shaped kiln bricks.

Excavated brick.

The back 3 rooms excavated by Alan.

Joyce Percival showed us a large Salt Jug dated 1862 which was a prize possession of one of the villagers. It showed a lovely oatmeal manganese glaze.

Visit with Mrs Joyce Chitty, (a leading member of the Northern Ceramic Society), on Wednesday, 8th November, 2006. Because of the poor weather conditions prevailing the washing of the shards by the village children had been cancelled so I took Joyce, (an ex deputy teacher, now retired), to Dearham school where the Headmistress Mrs Coates, the Deputy Head Mrs Cockcroft and class teacher Mrs McAdam made us most welcome.

I gave a talk to a class of children, approx., 9-10 years of age. The children were most attentive, well mannered and curious. I passed around various shards from the 19th century Fox House Farm Pottery site (which is quite near the Dearham site to which the children had paid a visit). The shards were of glazed and unglazed pieces of banded ware; a biscuit shard showed a centre moulding of a shamrock, a thistle and a rose together with 2 large crossed keys. I then passed amongst the children a large piece of lead ore mined in the nearby Newlands valley, near Keswick which had been used to glaze the nineteenth century pots. The Head Teacher then instructed a boy and girl to act as our guides to show us round their school. Joyce and I were impressed by a collage of 4 inch tiles on the back wall of their assembly hall. They made a centre border. It looked very attractive.

Joyce showing a shard.

Dearham School children in front of their collage of tiles.

162

FOX HOUSE (THE POT KILN) BROUGHTON MOOR

A Robert Wilson of Broughton Grange, West Cumberland owned the outlying coal mines Bertha, Alice, Dovenby, and Old Weasel. He had two sons of whom Lloyd was educated to become a mine manager whilst William was trained to become a farmer. Miss Edith Turnbull, school teacher and octogenarian told me her grandfather Mr Tom Turnbull was William's farm manager. Her father was the village policeman at Broughton Moor. It was Edith, now deceased, who allowed me to photograph her lovely toddy kettle and tobacco jar in the late 1970s which had been made at the Fox House pottery.

The tobacco jar is signed underneath 'John Docherty'. Both pots show a yellow clay body over which a manganese oxide glaze has been trickled, which gives a lovely effect. Fortunately when Miss Turnbull died both pots were purchased by the Helena Thompson Museum, in Workington.

The first potter recorded at Fox House Pottery was Jona Lister. When he christened his child at nearby Bridekirk Church, Broughton he described himself as a *Potter, Fox House*, on the church registers in 1802. He was followed by John Docherty. The pottery closed in 1880; however Fox House is farmed by the same Lister family to this day.

A popular selling product at Fox House pottery was the many children's money boxes, (in coarse earthenware). I recorded one which is initialled and dated A.F. 1836 and is 6 inches high with a moulded knob. I gather the coin slot was damaged when a rich uncle put half a sovereign into the box. The family being hard up, it became a matter of a *forced entry*. I was informed by the family that the rich uncle was the Great Broughton pipe manufacturer who eventually became one of the most eminent Cumberland scholars, Abraham Fletcher, noted in local directories for this period. It is now owned by a member of his family in West Cumberland.

Another money box I recorded is five inches high and has a moulded knob. It is decorated with a *capital 'D' with a heart shaped stamp on the opposite side to the coin slot* (Docherty?). The bases of neither money box are glazed. Mr Charles Nicholson, a Boot Boy at the nearby stately home of the Senhouse family *Netherhall Mansion* rescued a lovely spirit flask showing the same treacle glaze. Once thought to be boot warmers, they are now known to be spirit flasks.

During my many excavations at Fox House, mainly under the cow shed, I discovered a wonderful crisply moulded part-tureen shard in biscuit, showing large crossed keys; it also had a raised centre moulding which depicts a rose, thistle and a shamrock. Possibly a broken fragment of what was to be a dinner service for the House of Keys, in the Isle of Man. (Please note other Isle of Man items and shards in 'Teawares' page 64.

The Isle of Man was supplied with much of its pottery from the West Cumberland potteries and for decades the mines of West Cumberland had provided the island with domestic coal for the cold winter months. The island would also receive many visitors from West Cumberland for their annual holidays.

The shards from Fox House, when washed, proved the potters were meeting the domestic needs of the surrounding villages, their wares being nearly identical to those I have uncovered and recorded from the nearby Dearham and Clifton potteries which are all in the Allerdale area of West Cumberland.

Another point of interest in this Allerdale area was that most of the potteries had a *brick works* nearby as in Staffordshire. However this was not the case in the Copeland area of West Cumberland. The Whitehaven Brick and Tile Company is some way from the pottery sites but they shared the same source for coal and clay.

A cereal bowl shard, in biscuit, displayed the same potting characteristics as the marked cereal bowls made at the Whitehaven pottery and the same sponging technique of decoration i.e. the 'Potato pattern' in underglaze blue/white. The rim pips can also be seen on the handle of a (marked) Whitehaven pottery marriage puzzle jug. There is no doubt this form of domestic pottery would be made in the same way throughout the country at this period.

The quality of the Fox House pottery banded ware, fine stoneware shards was exceptional, both glazed and those in the biscuit. It proved they used a variety of colours, blue, green, white, brown and black on the bands which had been hardened on. The shards showed evidence of being thinly potted and beautifully turned. One could imagine a nice tobacco jar or vase decorated in this manner.

There were a great number of plant pot shards, dark iron oxide glazed, teapot shards and spittoons showing the shell moulding, whilst the dark red clay bowl shards showed the glaze had been used sparingly. A good proportion had unglazed bases. Others were slip decorated.

I remember one day chatting to elderly Bill Lister, the then owner of Fox House Farm. He recalled his grandfather the Potter telling him how he nearly finished up in the debtor's prison because rats had burrowed their way into his kiln. Time and again his pots had blistered! However an itinerant peddler who often bought his pots to sell on told the Potter this often happened in Staffordshire. Bill said the locals came and helped his grandfather sort out the rat problem with their terriers and fill in the holes in his kiln whilst their wives came and purchased his pots once again.

House of Keys shard, note the centre moulding of rose, thistle and shamrock.

Child's money box initialled A.F. for Abraham Fletcher, 1866.

A toddy kettle beautifully glazed.

Signed by J. Docherty, the Potter.

A second Manganese glazed Toddy Kettle.

Banded ware shards.

A second child's money box.

A hunt stirrup cup.

THE GINNS HOUSE POTTERY, WHITEHAVEN.
(known locally as the Brown Pottery)

The Ginns pottery is shown on *Matthias Read's* painting '*A Bird's Eye View of Whitehaven*', published in 1738 and again on *John Howard's* map of 1790 (see Volume 1, page 13, source C.R.O. Carlisle).

My research into the Lowther family documents at the C.R.O. in Carlisle provided me with the date this pottery began in 1740. Encouraged by Sir James Lowther it was managed by John Atkinson. *(Courtesy of the Lowther family trust)*.

A large crock for putting eggs into isinglass.

John Atkinson left the Ginns House pottery in 1756 and retired to Scilly Banks where he rented a cottage which was owned by the Lowther family but had previously been let to Aaron Wedgwood III who had gone to live and work at St. Bees for Peter How.

John Atkinson's successor at the Ginns House pottery was John Hudson. In 1779 he handed over to his son Peter who worked the pottery until 1796. Partners Henry Richardson and Joseph Benn then decided to take over the lease.

These men also leased a Stamp Mill at Bransty (no doubt for crushing glass, flints and stones, see Volume I, page 100). They not only produced coarse earthenware but Joseph Benn successfully contracted for work on the lands and tenements in Preston Quarter, for the Lowther estates.

According to the Shipping Intelligence lists for 1819 in the *Whitehaven Herald* (see Chapter II, page 57) a Joseph Richardson is recorded as shipping earthenware to America from the Ginns House Pottery, presumably Henry's son.

The Lowther records for 1834 show the Ginns House pottery is now in the ownership of John Kitchin.

In the 1960s an advertisement for Kitchin's shop shown at the local cinema portrayed a young waitress, wearing her black dress and white frilly cap and apron, carrying a tray of pots down the stairs – she tripped and the pots broke, the caption read:-

Flagon impressed H. Tyson.

'NEVER MIND THERE'S PLENTY MORE AT KITCHINS'.

His son John Junior did not follow his father into business. A religious man he became pastor of the Congregational Church at Woodhouse, Sheffield. John's daughter Sarah succeeded her father in the retail side of the business.

Mining records from the Barrow Mine at Newlands, Keswick mention that the mine supplied John Kitchin of the Ginns House Pottery with 2 tons 12cwts of Galena (potter's ore). In Chapter II, page 30 I record that John Tebay, of the Keswick Mines is mentioned as a partner in the Whitehaven Pottery. I also illustrate two types of potter's ores used in the glazing process. Galena is a very hard metal oxide however my sample of Cerrusite ore nearly disappeared in the very short time it was in my possession, it just crumbled away.

In 1854 the pottery was bought by Henry Tyson. Unfortunately his son Edward was drowned at Freemantle, Western Australia. Four years later Henry Tyson sold out to a Frederick Patman.

*The whereabouts of the Ginns House and Glass House potteries
are marked in yellow, top of the print (25)*

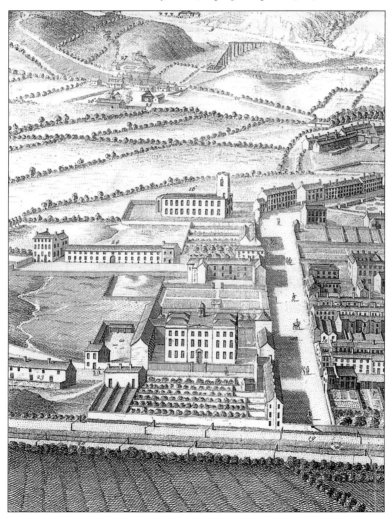

In the 1841 Whitehaven Census the Patman family were living in Queen Street, Whitehaven. The father Frederick is recorded as being a Customs Officer, at Whitehaven and son John was working as a clerk to John Wilkinson at the Whitehaven Pottery. Son Frederick is mentioned as being an apprentice potter to John Kitchin at the Ginns House Pottery.

Frederick Patman took control in 1858 and retired in 1880, finally handing over control to his nephew John Atkinson Patman, living at No. 13 Meadow View, Whitehaven.

John Thornber is recorded as Manager of the pottery from 1910 until it closed in 1915.

The print illustrated on page 167 shows the coal coming from the Lowthers' Howgill Coal Mines at Whitehaven and being taken nearly directly into the Ginns House and the Glass House potteries nearby. *(The coal conveyor system is shown as a wooden structure behind the two potteries which are marked in yellow at the top of the print)*

This detail is from Richard Parr's engraving of a 'Bird's Eye View of Whitehaven' by Matthias Read. (One example of this painting is in the Beacon Heritage Centre, Whitehaven. *Courtesy of Major Ray Devlin, Friends of Whitehaven Museum, who has written about the local coal mines).*

The Ginns House pottery was renowned for the quality of its brown ware items also

Dougie Mullen's part stoneware puzzle jug.

the lovely glazes which they achieved on their pots. However no one was more astonished than I, when the following item of pottery turned up. Found on the site of the Ginns pottery by Dougie Mullen. As a boy he visited the then owners of the site Mr and Mrs Joe Mossop. Dougie asked Aunt Emma if he could keep the remains of a puzzle jug. I rescued it just in time; Dougie's wife Dorothy was rather attracted to the moulding and thought she might get the top ground down. The family thought it would make an attractive vase for daffodils. The Whitehaven pottery nearby was being successful in the manufacture of puzzle jugs but *transfer printed ones*. So the Ginns House pottery decided to compete with them and make puzzle jugs in stoneware, with *sprigging.*

In Volume I of my book *'The History of The West Cumberland Potteries, Page 62,* I give details of the workload of the Caster at the Ginns House pottery, John Moncrief, with reference to his cutting and carting of the clay for the pottery. He also carted the finished pots to the ships in Whitehaven harbour that would transport them round the country and overseas. In addition he himself walked all over Cumberland to sell the pots, and only rode on his horse and cart when they were sold.

The picture on the right illustrates the condition of the roads which John Moncrief would have encountered before the turnpike roads were constructed.

THE GLASS HOUSE POTTERY, WHITEHAVEN
(known locally as the yellow pottery).

This started in 1813 when Sir William Lowther leased buildings in the Preston Street area of the Ginns, Whitehaven, to Joseph Goulding and John Tunstall of Little Broughton (son of the potter James of Broughton Moor) to begin a fourth pottery in the town.

The buildings were those of the now disused Glass Works started by Walter Ludwidge and Co., in the seventeenth century. The potters shared the premises with local school children. Rows of small cottages, with very basic amenities, had been built nearby by the Lowther family to

One of the Lake District passes encountered by John Moncrief. This one is 'Dunmail' Keswick to Ambleside.

house the miners and their families. Eventually a new school was built in 1876.

When Joseph Goulding died in 1827 a Francis Trousdale joined John Tunstall. The partnership lasted until John Tunstall died in 1860.

Francis Trousdale leased the pottery to potter Lewall Todd in 1873. Then a potter called James Kelly took it over in 1897.

A 'Bodger' used for pushing the clay into a mould. Given to the author by Mr Jack Soppit, of Whitehaven. It is inscribed 'J. Gill', and dated 12th Dec.,1845. It is made from the same material as a sagger.

Obviously this ex glass works site would sound inviting to the potters, as flints when calcined or burnt are used for making the beds for the ware to be fired. Being pure silica, it has the same melting properties and does not adhere to the ware (pots). Bowls and cups are put in the oval saggers whilst plates are fired separately in a bed of calcined flint which is formed round them in the required shape. The firing of the common brown earthenware is a fairly easy process.

Felspar now comes from Sweden in its present form. English and Irish flints are usually stained with iron. Raw Felspar is a salmon pink but when burnt, is pure white. The Glazer is a skilled man. He uses Cornish stone, borax and lead which is burnt in a 'fritt kiln' and once melted forms glass. In this state it is run into cold water and immediately disintergrates into small pieces thus making it easier for the Glazer to grind for his mix. This mixing process usually takes 10 days until it comes to a creamy consistency. The Glazer usually travelled from pottery to pottery.

A Window Stop or more likely one of a set of four Furniture Rests, to keep furniture off a damp flagged floor. (Courtesy of the Pitblade family of Kells, Whitehaven).

HARRINGTON POTTERY

Harrington is a small village with a port or harbour situated at the mouth of the beck or stream called the Wyre. It lies to the south of the town of Workington and was constructed by Henry Curwen of nearby Workington Hall. There were 43 vessels registered here and 1,900 persons residing in 350 houses, in 1828 according to local records in the C.R.O., Whitehaven.

Coal raised from the nearby small mines was exported in great quantities to Ireland, also lime to Scotland from the nearby quarries of Distington. Ironstone of an extremely superior quality was also exported to the iron foundries of Wales as well as fireclay upwards of 500 tons per year.

The records of Harrington Church for the year 1776 record Potter Daniel Simpson marrying local woman Mary Fisher on the 21st October.

An advertisement in the *Cumberland Pacquet* newspaper dated 30/08/1786 records 'Pot Kilns and Grounds, on the south side of the harbour at Harrington, late John Smith's rent £20 per year to let'.

The same newspaper dated Friday, 15th September, 1786, records

At the home of Joseph Stockdale in Harrington Harbour together or in parcels several freehold dwelling houses, pot kilns and grounds on the south side of the said harbour (late John Smiths) containing 40 yds in length of front and 20 yards backwards near the Wagon Way. These premises were lately let for £20 per annum and are capable of a good improvement at a small expenses.

Two years later in 1788 the same newspaper records 'Clay suitable for pottery and firebricks is being shipped to Jonathan Wainwright and Richard Bailiff of Liverpool'.

Up till now I have recorded no shards or pots from this site.

LADYPIT POTTERY, WHITEHAVEN
(known locally as the High Pottery).

The earliest record of this Ladypit pottery site which is now the well known pub the Sunnyhill Hotel is recorded on an indenture for the provision of a Hallow-ware Squeezer which can be seen in the Beacon Heritage Centre, Whitehaven. This legal document dated 1817 was drawn up between Mr Peter Woodnorth, a partner in the large Whitehaven Pottery at this time and an apprentice Watson Bell. (Hallow-ware objects are thrown items i.e. bowls, cups, jugs etc.) Watson Bell later became the foreman at Mr Kitchin's brown pottery in the Ginns.

Peter Woodnorth was in partnership in this venture with a Francis Davies. Mr Woodnorth left Whitehaven for Scotland 10 years later in about 1824. (see Chapter II).

The Ladypit pottery was advertised for sale in 1834 and taken over by the former apprentice Watson Bell and a man called Jackson. They advertised their ware as

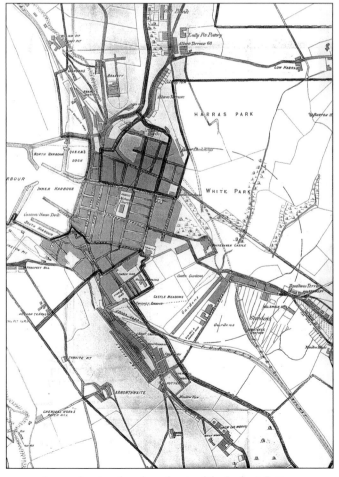

A map showing the whereabouts of the Ladypit Pottery.

ironstone, cane ware, blackglazed teapots, pomphry and grave vases, they also advertised vacancies for a few stout boys.

Plans for the Ladypit pottery (on the site of the present Sunnyhill Hotel.) These are dated 12th December, 1881.

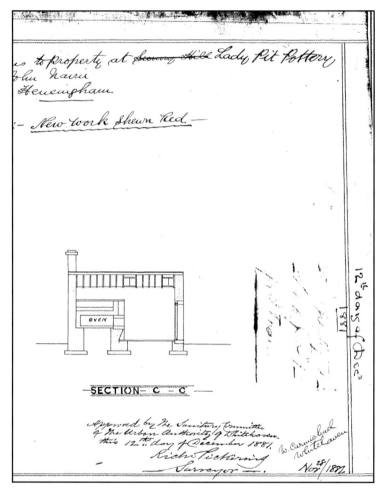

Courtesy of Susan Dench, a Senior Archivist C.R.O Carlisle.

An advertisement in a local paper in 1836 shows the partnership as Bell, Jackson and Miles Turner who also had shares in the large Whitehaven Pottery. Jackson retired on the 17th February, 1844 and the Ladypit Pottery was taken on by Mr Benjamen Walker. In 1850 a Ralph Smith took control. It closed sometime during this decade.

A Pilgrim Flask in the Beacon Collection shows the head of a young Queen Victoria, probably a Coronation souvenir 1838. (She became Queen in 1837).

An item of earthenware will pass through quite a few processes. Firstly the preparer of the clay, the baller, the thrower, the carrier, the turner, the biscuit firing, the dipper, the glost firing, a printer or painter and perhaps a gilder, the enamel firing and finally the burnisher. Then the sorter, packer and transporter so a large workforce is required.

They need many buildings; a Mill to grind the stone and flints, a Slip House where the clay is prepared, the proper pot shop where the thrower works, the Press Shop where everything from a Soup Tureen to a Teacup is made in a mould, a Kiln, the Dipping Room for glazing, finally a room for the Printer or Gilder. The gold comes from the nearest assay office in small pellets. This is used very sparingly. I'm sure much of the Whitehaven Gilding would be outside decorated.

THE LITTLE AND GREAT BROUGHTON POTTERIES

The Clifton, Rebton (now Ribton), Dearham Village and the Little and Great Broughton Potteries are all within a radius of 5 miles. Therefore the Listers, the Wedgwoods, Tunstalls and Ostle families were well acquainted with each other. These village potteries are separated only by the fine fishing river Derwent which flows from the nearest town Cockermouth to the sea at Workington. During the 18th and early 19th centuries it was an area rich in small coal seams under which lay the secondary clay for making earthenware.

Tim Malkin is recorded on the Bridekirk Church registers (the parish church), as working as a potter when baptising his son Rowland on the 21st October, 1727; however a Thomas Foorth was previously recorded as the potter in this area. These facts were researched by the staff of the C.R.O. in Carlisle for Mr Peter Brears, author of the book 'English Country Potters'.*

By 1773 local directories record James Tunstall as the potter. I am convinced James Tunstall made the *copy* of the Stephen Shaw inscribed dish, (known as the Clifton Marriage Dish) either here or at Dearham. The initials on this dish I.T. mean he had obtained the mould around 1767 for two inhabitants of the village of Great Broughton Edward Harrington and Mary Thompson. The back of the marriage dish shows the *impressed lettering* 'Clifton Dish' see Chapter I, page 7.

In 1813 his son John, who had been working as a part time potter and farmer at nearby Fox House, decided he would go into partnership with Joseph Goulding and start the Glass House pottery in Whitehaven (the yellow pottery) see Chapter IV page 169. A large imposing gravestone (situated on the pathway leading up to the Church at Brigham, near Cockermouth) is dedicated to the memory of John Tunstall's five children, *who all died in the year 1827*. John's name is included on the headstone. However, he didn't die until 1860. To date no marked pots have surfaced from this pottery.

Abraham Fletcher, pipe maker of Little Broughton (b.1714-d.1793) is recorded in Messrs Parson and Whites Directory of Cumberland and Westmorland under 'Eminent Men of Cumberland'. I wonder if the small money box initialled 'A.F. 1866', which had been made at the Fox House Farm pottery had been for a nephew or great grandson of

---

* *Courtesy of Peter Brears.*

the same name. This family heirloom belonged to the late Arthur Smith of Whitehaven who allowed me to photograph it in the 1980s.

Cumberland Pacquet 3/11/1807 C.R.O. Carlisle.
Little Broughton
House, pottery etc., situate at Little Broughton to let.

Cumberland Pacquet 1/06/1813
Monday at Crosscannonby Mr John Huddleston of Broughton Pottery to Mary Graham of Maryport.

MARYPORT POTTERY (GLASSON)

The pottery at Maryport was founded in 1752. A town plan of 1760 clearly shows the site of the pottery. On the 26th December that same year, a George Monkhouse of Penrith, a Wine Merchant, took a building lease (No. 33) of a 120 foot frontage onto King Street, Maryport.

A Sun Insurance policy for £500 taken out on the property records that it was occupied by the following men Mr Thomas Aydon, Mr James Miller, Mr Robert Lawson and Mr William Bragg & others. The buildings were insured as follows:-

A Clay Mill & 2 Pot Chambers (buildings) over it a Clay House & the Warehouse adjoining	350	0
A Kiln house & 2 pot chambers	50	0
Trade being Pots in ye Pot Chambers	100	0
Trade being Glass	1000	0
All ye said buildings being brick & stone built & slated.		
Total Premium	£2000	0

(Courtesy of Bruce Jones, Chief Archivist, Carlisle Record Office also Miss Bellis of the Kendal County Record Office).

This premium being charged for the Maryport Pottery & Glass Works, is equivalent to millions of pounds in today's money. To date no known pots or glassware have been recorded.

The Richard Lamplugh family of Dovenby owned the Rebton/Dearham Estates, near Maryport. Under the heading Maryport Glassworks, 1769, a George Monkhouse and a Richard Lewis took a lease for 21 years of the Senhouse Colliery, near Maryport which would supply the fuel necessary for the Maryport Glass and Pottery works. C.R.O. Carlisle.

The above lease also mentions a Robert Lawson who was later to become a Freeman of the city of Lancaster as a Sugar Refiner.

Later research by Mrs Elizabeth Adams recorded a list of Freeman of the City of Bristol (1767/68) where she found the name Robert Lawson, son of Robert (ex Maryport Pottery), and goes on to record a short passage from an article on *The Early Glasshouses of Bristol* by Francis Buckley, which draws the threads of the connection between Robert Lawson of Bristol and Lancaster with the glassworks and pottery at Maryport.

The Glass-makers of Bristol took their special knowledge of enamel glass into Ireland, Lancashire & elsewhere, and in these places founded prosperous glass-works.

Parson & White's *Directory of Cumberland & Westmorland, 1829* records Daniel Brough, course earthenware pottery near the Maryport harbour. Daniel was no doubt providing the local requirements for domestic pottery.

Maryport Harbour 1837.

The original engravings of these two photographs are on show in the Café area, at the Aquarium, in Maryport. Courtesy of the owner.

A ship trying to enter the harbour in a storm.

THE WIGTON POTTERY

The documents for this Wigton area are not easily accessible as they are held in safe keeping at Cockermouth Castle by the local landowner Lord Egremont, Lord of five towns and other Manors in West Cumberland. They must be requested from the County Archive Offices. Fortunately I had better luck going to Wigton Public Library. The Assistant was very helpful and pointed me in the direction of a book a local historian had published in 1993 about the history of the town, John Higham, who taught English at the Nelson Tomlinson Grammar School .

In the early 1970s, in the Tenters area of Wigton, he recorded finding mainly nineteenth century pottery shards and fragments of clay pipes.

Whilst in the Wigton Library I got into a conversation with an elderly lady. I explained why I was in the library. She told me about the Wigton potter who took pots into the prison in Carlisle. Business was good for him until a prisoner escaped hidden in the straw which he used for keeping his pots apart and the potter lost the order.

Michaelmas Petitions, C.R.O. Carlisle. 1742

No. 20 – Joseph Aglionby of Wigton, (Oulton).
> The Justice of the Peace Mr Briscoe recommends the parish to buy Mr Aglionby a Galloway Pony for him to resume his trade in earthenware.

In the Wigton parish registers we find that a William Smith, potter, christened a son William 1st January, 1780. Potter Charles Steward christened a son George 22nd February, 1789 and was still there in 1790. A James Lowther christened a daughter

Jane, 1st April, 1792. He was still there in 1796; Tolson Lowther also christened a son John. (John's name also appears on the St. Bees Church registers in 1790/1794) so Tolson must therefore have worked at the Ginns House pottery Whitehaven, at that time. Thomas Williamson christened a daughter Eleanor and registered himself as a potter in 1795. Potter James Young christened a daughter Sarah, (similarly he also appears in the St. Bees Church registers for 1793, so James must therefore, have also worked at the Ginns House pottery) at this period.

Sculpture of Gordon Boswell – the Travelling Pot Salesman who attends the
Annual Appleby Fair, in Westmorland.
Produced by Master Sculptor – Ray Ayres, of Border Fine Arts Ltd.

WETHERIGGS POTTERY, PENRITH

I want to just briefly mention this pottery in East Cumbria as Mrs Barbara Blenkinship, also the past owners Jonathan and Peter Snell, have written comprehensive guides illustrating the methods, machinery and pots which have been made at this pottery which specialised mainly in producing slip decorated wares.

It started in 1855 as a brickyard and tilery for the Lord Brougham Estate however ten years later it was taken over by the Scofield family of potters, of Newcastle on Tyne (The Stepney Bank Pottery). The Brougham Estate was sold off in 1932, so the Scofield family bought the pottery. Ten years later 90,000 items a year were being produced most of these going through Lake District shops or retail outlets. In 1973 the pottery was scheduled as an Industrial Monument and is still a working pottery today carrying on the tradition of producing slipware items.

Overleaf is a photograph of the rim of a slip decorated puzzle jug which belonged to D. Thorburn, a direct ancestor of the recipient, (the brother of Mrs Proud, nee Scofield of Cleator Moor, West Cumbria).

It has a manganese oxide glaze which extends practically to its base. It is slip decorated and dated 1856, reticulated with a diamond cut. It is 8½ inches in height and 17½ inches in width around the centre body. The large handle comes out approx., 3 inches from the main body. The rim is slip decorated with horizontal lines and dots to the inside. The handle is slip decorated in a snaking zig zag line in interspersed with dots.

The rim of the puzzle jug which is in the ownership of Mrs Proud's brother in Penrith.

A variety of glazed jugs. Family favourites and heirlooms especially the blue slipt ones.

On the left a cobalt blue glazed fruit bowl.
On the right two slip glazed egg cups with the mark clearly identified.

A lovely blue glazed jug with a white slipt interior, another family heirloom

WHITEHAVEN POTTERY, THE HISTORY OF PRINTS ON THE CHILDREN'S PLATES AND DARNING EGGS:

GIFTS FOR GOOD CHILDREN – THE HISTORY OF CHILDREN'S CHINA 1790-1890 by Noel Riley. Book I was published by Richard Dennis, in 1991.

When I bought this book, it kept me interested for weeks. It records over 800 prints on children's plates and small mugs, the collection of Richard Dennis, and records their history. For the sake of ceramic research they have allowed me to quote from some of their records so that we can begin to understand the similarities and differences on the Whitehaven prints and shards, I have recorded to date, compared to those of other pot banks. There are still no pots, (up-to-now) for some of these shards!

Herewith fourteen Whitehaven pottery patterns which were printed on their children's plates and darning eggs which I have recognised from Noel Riley's illustrations.

EARLY DAYS
The Romp, No. 136, Page 49 in Noel Riley's book.

Riley reckons that the source for this illustration was first issued as an aquatint circa 1828-30 and subsequently published in lithograph form under the title *Our Early Days* by W. Clerk, 202 High Holborn, circa 1840. Riley records three plates depicting this print, two of which are unmarked, whilst one is marked with an indecipherable blob.

I have recorded this print on a Whitehaven pottery Darning Egg (*a bat print*) and also on a child's plate in creamware which shows a border moulding of enamelled foliage and sprays of flowers over the glaze, whilst a third item is a one pint frog mug blue/white underglaze printed. The frog inside the mug is painted green and is well sculptured.

The Pet, – No. 137, Page 49 in Noel Riley's book.

Riley's plate shows the same centre print as the one on the Whitehaven factory Darning Egg (a *bat print*). She shows that the ceramic painter has completely ignored the border moulding and instead decorated the rococo border with a variety of over glaze enamelled flowers - roses, tulips, and asters.

Two young girls leaving school share an umbrella – No. 149, page 50 in Riley's book.

According to Noel Riley the print source is *The Mother's Pictorial Alphabet*. A print depicted on our Whitehaven pottery Darning Eggs which is black printed.

Boys flying their kite – No. 202, page 63 in Noel Riley's book.

According to Noel Riley the print source is once again *The Mother's Pictorial Alphabet*.

This print is recorded on a Whitehaven pottery Darning Egg. A shard was excavated on the Whitehaven pottery site in 1987 by boy helpers from St. Bees School; it depicts paper bows tied to the kite string. This was illustrated in *The History of the West Cumberland Potteries,* Volume I, Figure 1, page 38, published in 1991.

STEAM AND WIND POWER
Train coming out of a tunnel, No. 574, page 159, in Noel Riley's book.

She reckons the plate illustrated is printed in green and records the train to be a 2-2-2 passenger locomotive.

A Lord of the realm owns a Whitehaven Darning Egg and also a child's plate, both show this print. He is a rail enthusiast and confirmed the Whitehaven train to be the one recorded by Noel Riley. Whitehaven pottery Darning Eggs depicting this print have been recorded in sepia whilst another is under glaze black printed.

OCCUPATIONS AND TRADES
The Newsboy – No. 622, page 167 in Noel Riley's book.

A Mother's Alphabet print which Riley's records as being of a granular nature.

The Whitehaven factory made a Darning Egg depicting this print in sepia, could this be the granular nature recorded by Noel Riley? Another is recorded which depicts *The Newsboy* pattern under glaze black printed.

FLORA AND FAUNA
Jack's Birthday – No. 756, page 197 of Noel Riley's book.

Noel Riley records this plate to be unmarked, and goes on to say it is straight edged with a moulding of shamrocks, roses and thistles and reckons the print has been recorded on a plate with a lustred border and a green centre print.

At the NEC Antiques Fair, Birmingham, 2005 I discovered a Whitehaven creamware child's plate, the centre underglaze printed in green showing the print *Little Titty*. See the photograph on page 118.

A third plate recorded by Riley shows this same centre print in black with a border of sprigs of foliage painted in red and green enamels.

Excavations on the Whitehaven site revealed many shards of this print in various colours (see photograph on page 126), however the Whitehaven shards show the wording *JACK'S BIRTHDAY* below the centre print, whereas Riley's plate No. 756 the wording is shown above the centre print.

I'm fairly certain this third plate, recorded by Noel Riley, was made at Whitehaven. The border description is identical to that depicted on *The Young Charioteer* for which we have shards, whilst our small creamware plates printed with *Now I'm a Grandmother, Keeping School* and *The Romp*, all depict the same border of sprigs of foliage painted in vivid red, green and blue enamels.

The Young Nurse, No. 140, page 49 in Riley's book,

A large earthenware Darning Egg shard was recently excavated by a local man Tony Calvin, which depicted *The Young Nurse* print in black/white. I had previously recorded a whole Darning Egg in this pattern underglaze printed in black.

FLORA AND FAUNA

Beggar's Petition, No. 775, page 202 in Noel Riley's book.

Noel Riley reckons the plate illustrated to be unmarked and goes on to say that the plate has been recorded with a vitruvian scroll and alphabet border. Riley records that the *Beggars Petition* is a pious poem by Moss.

The Whitehaven factory adapted this print to a much more frivolous idea.

I have now recorded three Whitehaven pottery objects which show this print. One was a small child's mug. The print on the reverse is an unrecorded print *The First Nibble*; luckily we had excavated 2 shards, one in sepia and one in under glaze blue/white.

The second item was an earthenware child's plate showing this *Beggar's Petition* print, the border moulding is of hanging garlands of flowers. which I have illustrated on page 118.

I discovered a third item, a child's plate, in creamware, at the N.E.C. Antiques Fair, Birmingham, 2005; it depicts this *Beggar's Petition* print, under glaze printed in pink. The border shows a moulding of florets which are separated by a moulding of raised dots in a variety of patterns.

Little Titty – No. 799, page 207 in Noel Riley's book

She states that the plate illustrated is unmarked and goes on to describe it, *a rococo edge which is painted dark red, the border is of moulded flower sprigs the sepia print shows a little girl with her kitten. (See front cover of* The History of The West Cumberland Potteries, *Volume I, published 1991).*

Since then I have discovered a creamware child's plate *Little Titty* at the N.E.C. Antiques Fair, Birmingham, in 2005. The border moulding is of rose, tulip and aster, the centre is under glaze printed in green. Research has enabled me to record other small Whitehaven plates with this identical border moulding, some overglaze enamelled in vivid red, green and blue. The print is also recorded on our Whitehaven Darning Eggs, black printed. An earthenware child's plate has recently been recorded with this centre print *Little Titty;* however it shows a rare *fish scales* moulded border for which we have excavated shards, in biscuit.

Girl Feeding Her Rabbits – No. 843, page 215 in Noel Riley's book.

Noel Riley quotes from the Mother's Pictorial Alphabet. '*R begins Rosa: how pleased she appears. To watch those plump Rabbits with long silky ears*'.

This print is also depicted on the Whitehaven Darning Eggs; it is black printed.

PIETY AND VIRTUE

Begging Alms – No. 775, page 258 in Noel Riley's book.

Noel Riley reckons the plate she illustrates is unmarked; it depicts a ragged boy accompanied by a young girl. They are receiving bread from a lady who is leaning over a wall; the centre scene is black printed, it has a blue sponged border.

This is one of the Whitehaven pottery's most popular prints, named *Charity*. It is illustrated on the factory's darning eggs, tobacco jars, dinner plates, jug and bowl sets and our puzzle jugs. It is recorded underglaze printed in a variety of colours i.e. brown/white, black/white and blue/white. It is recorded with the early mark I.W. then later on, J.W. and also Warranted Stone China. The sponging technique which Noel states is on the border of her plate is recorded on pots made at the Whitehaven pottery and at Fox House Farm pottery, Broughton Moor, where fragments were excavated. .

ENTERTAINMENT
The Organ Grinder, No. 627, page 169 in Noel Riley's book.

She states this plate is unmarked and the print source to be from *Mother's Pictorial Alphabet.*

This print is depicted on a Whitehaven Darning Egg, in mulberry; another factory Darning Egg is decorated with an under glaze black print.

EARLY DAYS
Now I'm Grandmother, No. 135, on Page 49 in Noel Riley's book.

She claims the plate to be unmarked.

Once again this print *Now I'm Grandmother* is on a Whitehaven Darning Egg whilst the print *Little Titty* is on the reverse. I have now recorded a creamware child's plate with this print and a border of enamelled sprigs.

Royal Favourite's

A child's plate is illustrated by Rosalind Pulver in the *Antiques Dealer and Collectors Guide*, Dec., 1998. I have illustrated it together with one of our large shards on page 124.

We excavated many large shards, glazed and unglazed, which I reported in the N.C.S quarterly Newsletter some time ago regarding this pattern

CHAPTER V

CHRONOLOGICAL HISTORY OF POTTING IN WEST CUMBERLAND

SEVENTEENTH CENTURY

1637 Thomas Foorth, potter registers the birth of his son Henry, on the 23/04/1637. Dearham Parish Records, Bridekirk, page 39, C.R.O Carlisle.

1672 Andrew Pelin's Map of Whitehaven shows Hodgson's Croft. The Street maps of Whitehaven 1662-1743, D/Lons./W.162, (1742 page 76). indexed 1716. Later referred to as Douglas Burn. The 'Andrew Pelin Map', courtesy of Mr Blake Tyson, Oxford Polytechnical College.

1674 Edward Gibson, Whitehaven, potter, is making bricks, tiles and baking pots between the tiles. Courtesy of Prof. D.R. Ainsworth, Australia. The Records of Social and Economic History, New Series VII' A.M.S. Transactions, The Early Development of Whitehaven Before 1700. C.RO. Carlisle.

1686 Sir John Lowther's Agent writes him saying he thought Barrow full of maggots. He is proved correct. Barrow leaves Whitehaven leaving debts! C.R.O. Carlisle, Lowther Records same source as above.

1687 The tenaments in Hodgson's Croft are taken by a builder, a French gunsmith (takes 2 houses), a potter, a brick maker cum tiler and a French pipe maker. D/Lons./W.2/1/23/21. C.R.O. Carlisle. Courtesy of the Lowther family Trustees.

1689 Mr Jeremy Lyons, a potter, from Rainhill, Liverpool comes to Whitehaven, and a lease for 7 years is agreed; however he too leaves the area shortly after. Same source. C.R.O. Carlisle. Courtesy of the Lowther Family Trustees.

1694 Sir John Lowther subsidises Abel Robinson and a Frenchman, John Boulain to make tobacco pipes in Hodgson's Croft, (see copy of documents on page 3, Chapter 1, Seventeenth Century). These documents are courtesy of the Lowther family trustees, C.R.O. Carlisle.

1698 Aaron Wedgwood, a potter, is engaged, (from Staffordshire) to make trials at Aikbank, Whitehaven. These were unsuccessful. However Aaron did not go

SEVENTEENTH CENTURY – *Continued*

back to Staffordshire, he joined the potters of nearby (Rebton) now known as Ribton, Camerton near Cockermouth. It was here he found romance, and married Margaret Tunstall, a lady's maid.

1699   John Beck, Potter, Whitehaven baptises his daughter at St. Nicholas Church 26th May, 1699. St. Nicholas Church records, C.R.O.,Whitehaven.

1699   John son of Aaron and Margaret Wedgwood (nee Tunstall) is born at Rebton (now Ribton) according to the Bridekirk Church registers. Phillip Wedgwood, who compiled the Cumberland Wedgwood family tree, reckons John was born, or baptised, on the 19th November, 1699 and died in 1780.

EIGHTEENTH CENTURY

1701   Thomas son of Aaron and Margaret Wedgwood (nee Tunstall) baptised 24th July, Bridekirk Church registers.

1703   Margaret daughter of Aaron and Margaret Wedgwood (nee Tunstall) baptised 25th July, same source.

1704   Aaron son of Aaron and Margaret Wedgwood (nee Tunstall) born 12th January, same source.

1706   Mary Anne a daughter of Aaron and Margaret Wedgwood (nee Tunstall) baptised 2nd August, same source.

1708   Aaron Wedgwood and his wife Margaret start their own pottery at Harker Marsh, Broughton Moor, at Whistling Syke. Alan Harrison of Dearham recovered the door lintel which was inscribed A.M.W. 1708. This is now in the Helena Thompson Museum, Workington.

1709   Richard a son of Aaron and Margaret Wedgwood (nee Tunstall) baptised 15th January, same source.

1712   Moses a son of Aaron and Margaret Wedgwood (nee Tunstall). He died 1780, (same source).

1717   Thomas Wilson, Potter, Whitehaven, christens his son Archibald. 6th September, 1717. St. Nicholas Church records, C.R.O. Whitehaven.

1719   Timothy son of Aaron and Margaret Wedgwood (nee Tunstall) baptised 19th January, Bridekirk Church registers.

1720   The Wedgwood and Tunstall families of Dearham were extracting clay at Dearham. Recorded by Hugh Tait, ex Curator, the British Museum.

1724   Aaron Wedgwood senior is renting Dearham Manor, C.R.O Carlisle.

EIGHTEENTH CENTURY – *Continued*

1725 The date Stephen Shaw inscribed on the reverse of the slipware Marriage Dish now housed in the British Museum which according to the sale catalogue was sold at the closure of the Distington Private Museum in Cumberland. (see Chapter I, page 6).

1727 Tim Malkin, Potter, baptised his son Rowland on the 21st October C.R.O, Whitehaven, Bridekirk parish church reg. The name Malkin is well known in Staffordshire. William Wedgwood, master potter married Dorothy Malkin. A John Malkin is recorded as a witness to his Uncle Gilbert Wedgwood's will 20th January, 1666 (see *History of the Wedgwood family* by Josiah Clement Wedgwood M.P. 1299-1908) British Library.

1731 Moses, Thomas and Aaron II (of Cumberland born 1704) take out a lease on Dearham Mill and Kiln, 15/-s half yearly rent, document shows them still paying in 1738 to 1740. This was reduced to 12/-s. from 1741-44 C.R.O. Carlisle, Lowther Rentals Page 169. Courtesy of the Lowther family Trustees.

1732 Aaron Wedgwood III (of Cumberland) born at Dearham on the 25th June.

1733 Joseph Ashley, Potter, Whitehaven died 7/02/1733 St. Nicholas Church registers C.R.O. Whitehaven.

1738 Aaron Wedgwood senior is recorded as renting Dearham Mill. Courtesy of the Lowther family trustees. C.R.O. Carlisle.

1740 John Atkinson starts the Ginns House Pottery (the brown pottery) in Whitehaven. However, according to Lowther records, in 1754 he retired to the Scilly Banks cottage taking over the lease from the idle Aaron Wedgwood III.

1742 Joseph Aglionby is recorded as potting in Wigton, C.R.O. Carlisle.

1743 William Cockbain, St Bees, potter, married Abigail Borodale according to the St. Bees Church registers. This potter later went into partnership with Peter Woodnorth. They eventually took over the John Douglas pottery in Whitehaven. Cockbain retired at the end of the century whilst Peter Woodnorth went on to begin the large Whitehaven pottery in 1812 and the Ladypit pottery in 1813.

1754 Aaron Wedgwood III of Cumberland was invited to the Scilly Banks to make the red and creamware. He signed a lease permitting him to take clay from four commons namely, Distington, Preston Quarter, Moresby and Hensingham for 21 years (until 1775). C.R.O. Carlisle, courtesy of the Lowther family Trustees.

1754 R.R. Angerstein, the Swedish industrial spy, visited Whitehaven. (Page 280 in the Book of his travels published by The Science Museum, 2002).

1757 Aaron Wedgwood III married local girl Mary Dixon at St. James Church, Whitehaven, 27/12/1757. (Church registers C.R.O. Whitehaven). The Ester

EIGHTEENTH CENTURY – *Continued*

Saul creamware teapot shows her initials M.D. between the grass and handle finial (see photograph Chapter I, page 17).

1757   The Maryport Pottery started 26th December, 1757. C.R.O., Carlisle also The Northern Ceramic Society articles published by Elizabeth Adams.

1761   Aaron III and Mary Wedgwood (nee Dixon) baptise a son Aaron junior at Holy Trinity Church, Whitehaven, 1st, March, 1761. Church records C.R.O. Whitehaven.

1762   In the census of Whitehaven, 1762, also Lowther records for 1783 John Douglas is recorded as a potter, Market Place, Whitehaven (see Chapter II, page 22, ref. Lowther family documents.) Courtesy of the Lowther family Trustees.

1763   Peter How, who was employing Aaron Wedgwood at Low Mill, St. Bees went bankrupt.

1763   John Douglas lived in a house belonging to Mrs Blencowe, Market Place, Whitehaven. C.R.O. Whitehaven.

1764   Aaron Wedgwood III and Mary christen a son Moses, at St. Bees Church, (church registers), (the address given is a very desirable residence) Low Mill, St. Bees, the date 29/02/1764. St. Bees Church records C.R.O. Whitehaven.

1765   Aaron III and Mary christen a daughter Martha at St. Bees Church, address, once more is Low Mill, St. Bees, the date is 25th August, 1765, (same source).

1767   The Clifton Marriage Dish, is initialled by James Tunstall for the marriage of Edward Harrington and Mary Thompson. They lived in Broughton village.

1769   Susannah Drewry, creamware teapot is inscribed and dated 1769.

1770   The date inscribed on the Sam Abbot and Margrett Bowman creamware teapot. They are married 16th September, 1770 at St. Bees Church. Courtesy of Local History Librarian, Anne Dick, Whitehaven.

1770   Michael Collins, potter of Whitehaven paid a Sun Life premium of £6. Vol. 176-246651 Ladyday 1170. Elizabeth Adams.

1771   Midsummer, Michael Collins of Whitehaven paid a premium for a dwelling house and warehouse to the Sun Life Insurance Company Vol. 198. Elizabeth Adams, Guildhall Library, M.S. 11936 N.C.S. 'Echoes and Reflections' publication.

1771   Ester Saul (inscribed creamware teapot), she married, 7th March, (see Chapter II, page 18).

1772   Peter How dies. He is buried in St. Nicholas Church yard in Whitehaven. St. Nicholas church registers, C.R.O. Whitehaven; also documents at the Beacon, Whitehaven.

EIGHTEENTH CENTURY – *Continued*

1772 Documents from U.S.A. Retailer claiming that in a consignment of Whitehaven pottery, the small butter tubs are too fragile! (Professor George Miller and Asst. Professor Dr Anne Smart Martin, Winterthur University, U.S.A.).

1772 Thomas Pennant visited Whitehaven on his way to Scotland and recorded seeing Whitehaven pottery being loaded onto ships bound for the I.o.M. and America.

1773 John Douglas married Jane Crookshanks on the 13th March and takes over the lease of a shop, warehouse and dwelling house, under one roof, in the tenure of Henry Watts, Market Place, Whitehaven. C.R.O. Whitehaven.

1773 According to Bridekirk church registers James Tunstall, is living at the Little Broughton Pottery, the address he records when baptising his daughter. C.R.O. Carlisle.

1773 The Molly Drewry creamware teapot is inscribed and dated 1773.

1774 Aaron Wedgwood III and Mary christen a son Phillip, at St.Michael's Church Workington, Reg. 1750-90. Seemingly they have now left Low Mill, St. Bees.

1776 Aaron Wedgwood III and Mary (nee Dixon) baptise a son Peter 16th March, at St. Michael's Church, Workington. C.R.O. Whitehaven.

1776 Daniel Simpson, potter, Harrington, married Mary Fisher on the 21st October. C.R.O. Whitehaven.

1777 The Dearham village pottery. A dated shallow bowl, in 2 sections, treacle glazed dated 1777 and initialled J.P. bought by the Workington Museum for £400 plus; at Mitchells Auction Co., Cockermouth in 1992. Another was sold at Messrs. Penrith, Kydd and Farmers Auctioneers, Penrith in Dec., 2000, a 'telephone bidder' bought it for £360 plus. I know of one other dated 1855 and initialled W B see photo page 151 headed 'Dearham Pottery'.

1778 Daniel Douglas, Whitehaven, pot seller marries Catherine Taylor of Burslem, Staffordshire, N.C.S. Newsletter.

1779 William Wilberforce visits Whitehaven (the anti slavery campaigner).

1780 Frances Wedgwood, a daughter is baptised 13th February. parents Aaron Wedgwood and Mary at St. Michael's Church Workington, C.R.O. Whitehaven.

1780 Elizabeth Skelly marries James Mallet, potter on the 30th January. St. Bees Church registers, C.R.O. Whitehaven.

1780 Rachael Murray married Garry Johnston, Potter on the 24h April. at St. Bees Church, witnesses James Johnston and William Chisholm potter, St. Bees Church registers, C.R.O. Whitehaven.

EIGHTEENTH CENTURY – *Continued*

1781 Thomas Wedgewood a son, is baptised, parents Aaron Wedgwood and Mary 24th June St. Michael's Church registers, C.R.O. Whitehaven.

1783 William Wedgwood a son, is baptised at Camerton Church, parents Aaron Wedgwood and Mary. Records, P.R.143/2. They are now living at Seaton. (I find it quite strange that there is a 9 year gap between their first 3 children and the next 5!)

1783 Lowther documents showing John Douglas paying rent for a section of the Old Hall in Whitehaven to Mr John Gale. (courtesy of Lowther family Trustees).

1786 An advertisement in the Cumberland Pacquet newspaper dated 1786 reads Pot Kilns and ground on the Harrington harbour, late John Smiths for rent. C.R.O. Carlisle

1791 The Reverend John Wesley dies. I have recorded 3 items displaying this date of 1791, namely the I.M. (Isaac Moore) Tobacco Jar, the Bulb Pot inscribed with the initials P.H.N. and dated. Also the important wasters depicting The Rev. John Fletcher who was being trained to succeed the Rev. John Wesley. The fragments are of small children's plates; they depict his portrait and name, whilst underneath the caption reads March, 1791, London. This was reported to N.C.S. members in the Quarterly Newsletter.

1791 Daniel Douglas of Whitehaven is a witness at the wedding of John McKie, potter, on the 11th April. Entry 26, St. Nicholas Church registers, C.R.O. Whitehaven.

1797 Miss Reed daughter of Ebeneezer Reed, potter, marries at St. James Church, Whitehaven. C.P. 21/03/1797.

NINETEENTH CENTURY

1802 Jonah Lister of Fox House (the Pot Kiln) christens his daughter on the 7th January, 1802 and describes himself as a potter. on the Bridekirk Church registers. A sprigged tobacco jar bears the name of another potter at Fox House, John Docherty. John Tunstall is back here to live having left Whitehaven. George Brough, potter (probably the son of the coarse earthenware potter, Daniel, of Maryport.) married Rebecca Lister, aged 19, her address Pot Kiln, Fox House Farm. (Bridekirk church registers, C.R.O. Carlisle) The Lister family still own this farm today.

1807 Cumberland Pacquet Newspaper 3/11/1807 Little Broughton, House and pottery etc., situate at Little Broughton to let.

1810 Cumberland Pacquet newspaper 16/11/1810

The business carried on under the name Peter Woodnorth and Co., as China and

NINETEENTH CENTURY – *Continued*

Glass manufacturers was this day dissolved by mutual consent, all debts due and by the said firm will be recovered, and paid by Peter Woodnorth. Signed in the presence of David Rees, junior, Peter Woodnorth, John Hall and Ralph Hall of Staffordshire. (Whitehaven Museum Records.)

These also claim that clay was being brought in from Louth, Ireland. D.Hay late Curator,Whitehaven Museum.

1811   Mary Wedgwood wife of Aaron III, dies 10th December, 1811. Camerton Church records. C.R.O. Carlisle. They are living at Seaton and are retired.

1812   Aaron Wedgwood III of Cumberland dies. Aaron must have gone to live with his daughter at Flimby when he lost his wife. His death is recorded on Flimby P.R. 124/40, Burials, 2nd February, 1812. C.R.O. Carlisle. He was 83 years of age. Not only did the potter who made the Bulb Pot, (an 80th birthday present), get the date wrong, but once more, inscribed it E.W. instead of A.W! It is a Wedgwood family heirloom.

1812   The large Whitehaven pottery starts, the partners are Peter Woodnorth, local banker Joseph Harrison and Mr John Hall master potter of Staffordshire.

1813   Miss Mary Graham, Maryport marries John Huddleston, potter of Broughton pottery. The marriage took place at Crosscannonby Church, according to the Cumberland Pacquet Newspaper lst June, 1813.

1813   John Tunstall starts the Glass House pottery, Whitehaven. His large imposing gravestone in Brigham churchyard also records the tragic death of 5 of his children in 1827.

1817   The Ladypit pottery is started by Mr Peter Woodnorth.

1819   Shipping lists of pottery in the Whitehaven Gazette newspaper 1819-20.

1820   John Wilkinson takes over as Manager of the Whitehaven Pottery.

1822   John Wilkinson marries Mary Ann (nee Hall) at Burslem, in Staffordshire. She was the daughter of John Hall, master potter and a partner in the Whitehaven Pottery. On this occasion John Hall handed over his shares to the couple who took control whilst Peter Woodnorth, another partner left and went to manage the Verriville pottery at Finniston, Scotland.

1836   Documents refer to a consignment of earthenware to U.S.A.

1857   Carlisle pottery starts.

1861   Clay Flatts pottery is recorded.

1865   Wetheriggs pottery starts.

1882   A change of ownership, of the Whitehaven Pottery, is recorded in The Whitehaven

NINETEENTH CENTURY – *Continued*

News 25th May, 1882. The Whitehaven pottery company had been formed. The directors being Mr T. Brown, Mr J.G.Dees and Mr Paitson and the price paid was £10,000.

TWENTIETH CENTURY

1915 New owners Mr and Mrs Samuel West (a local butcher) turned the Whitehaven Pottery into the town's abattoir. It is sold to Mr and Mrs Tom Mossop in 1955 who then trade as builders' merchants. The Mossop family are still trading today.

MARKS

W.H.H. WHITEHAVEN	Whitehaven Pottery, underglaze transfer printed for the partnership Woodnorth, Harrison and Hall, date 1812-1820, in black.
WOODNORTH and CO.	Incised into the clay Woodnorth & Co., Whitehaven Pottery 1812-1820.
WOODNORTH'S WHITEHAVEN	Whitehaven Pottery, small capitals in a circle for Peter Woodnorth & Co., date 1812-1820 underglaze transfer printed in black.
W. and Co.	Whitehaven Pottery for Woodnorth & Co., 1812-1820 incised into the clay.
MARSEILLAISE I.W.	Whitehaven Pottery, Pattern name and initials within a ribbon scroll transfer printed underglaze in black/white, grey/white, pink/white and blue/white 1820-1924 John Wilkinson.

This mark was recently discovered on a pot with the pattern name Pet Lamb.

Underglaze printed on base of a saucer. Also the initials IW (John Wilkinson 1820-24).

W.P.Co WHITEHAVEN	Whitehaven Pottery Lettering within an oval border in a black underglaze transfer printed 1872-1915.	WARRANTED STONE CHINA I.W.	Whitehaven Pottery, Crown above a scroll with name contained inside in underglaze blue and white transfer printed John Wilkinson 1820-1824 also initials IW under scroll.
CHARITY J.W.	Whitehaven Pottery Pattern name with initials underneath both contained within a heart shaped foliated wreath in underglaze transfer printed blue/white or black/white. John Wilkinson. 1824-1868.	JOHN WILKINSON WHITEHAVEN WILKINSONS POTTERY Co. WHITEHAVEN	Whitehaven Pottery a stamp moulded mark 1824-1868. Whitehaven Pottery, name transfer printed in a circle. 1872-1915.
MAYFIELD I.W.	Whitehaven Pottery, floral wreath, initials underneath Underglaze blue/white transfer printed John Wilkinson (shard). 1820-1824.	R. WILKINSON WHITEHAVEN	Whitehaven Pottery Incised into the clay a stamp moulded mark, Randle Wilkinson 1868-1872.
		Signature John Docherty Broughton Moor	Broughton Moor Fox House Farm Pottery, incised into the clay 19th century.
STONE CHINA also an impressed star	Whitehaven Pottery Initials and category within a heavily lined block in in underglaze blue and white transfer print 1820-1824.	Clifton Dish	Hand written incised into the clay – Crossbarrow Pottery, Clifton, near-Workington, Cumbria. 18th century.

Whitehaven Pottery patterns

Pattern	Description	Rarity
Antiquities	Pale blue/white.	Rare
Amoy	One cup and saucer only. It is unique. Marked and initialled, printed in flow blue with a chinoiserie design.	Rare
Asiatic Pheasant	Underglaze printed in blue/white, green/white and brown/white.	Uncommon

Pattern	Description	Rarity
Albion Pattern	Underglaze printed in blue/white.	Uncommon
Batchelor's Set	Museum items.	Rare
Baker's Oven	Underglaze printed in green/white and grey/white. This pattern and the Bottle pattern also Loretto, all have the same border print and show the same identical impressed star factory mark on the reverse, plus shards.	Uncommon
Banded Ware	Mainly stoneware and earthenware items with bands of colour in various widths, hardened on around the item.	Uncommon
Bohemia	Printed in underglaze pale blue/white. One plate turned up in 2007.	Rare
The Bottle	Underglaze printed in green/white	Uncommon
Brosely	Underglaze printed in pale blue/white. Recorded in soft paste porcelain and earthenware.	Uncommon
Bosphorous	Underglaze printed in blue/white. Recorded in earthenware only up to date.	Uncommon
Brindley (James)	An earthenware desert plate has been recorded by Dr. G. Godden in his book *Encyclopaedia of British Pottery and Porcelain in the Appendix*. He records the plate is signed and dated with the factory mark of W. & Co. on the reverse.	Unique
Cyrene	Underglaze printed in pale blue/white. I have recorded no whole pots to date.	Shards only
Charity	Underglaze printed in blue/white and brown/white. It is depicted on a tobacco jar, jug and bowl sets etc.	Uncommon
Commemorative	Items recording Queen Victoria's Coronation. Events at local churches. The Isle of Man tourist trade items etc.	Rare items
Drunkard's Doom	Temperance movement items, underglaze printed in blue/white or grey/white.	Uncommon

Pattern	Description	Rarity
Erin	Excavated shards in blue/white and brown/white. Cup and saucer is recorded, underglaze printed in brown/white by Michael Berthoud in his collection in the 'Alton Museum', Hampshire.	Rare
Eastern Scenery	One large ashet is recorded up to date printed in underglaze blue/white.	Uncommon
First Nibble	A newly recorded pattern underglaze printed in black/white, with high temperature enamels, on a child's mug.	Rare
Frog Mugs	These Whitehaven frogs are well moulded.	Uncommon
Fruit	Underglaze printed in pink.	Uncommon
Free Trade	Underglaze printed in black/white.	Uncommon
Khartoum	Once again an incorrect spelling by the factory workman. Under glaze printed in brown/white, recorded on an ashet, with the factory mark of W.P.Co. (Whitehaven Pottery Co.).	Unique
Lowther	See N.C.S. Newsletter No. 16 re the Hillis Bowl. Two plates underglaze printed in blue/white are recorded in this pattern which the author has named.	Rare
Moss Rose	An under glaze print in blue/white; however a large shard was excavated in brown/white. The Minton factory also produced this pattern.	Uncommon
Mandarin with long pipe.	An underglaze print in pale blue/white produced by the Whitehaven and Glamorgan factories. Named by Helen Hallesey.	Rare
Minstrel	Underglaze blue/white printed plate.	Rare
Marseillaise	Underglaze printed in blue/white, pink/white, brown/white and flow blue.	Uncommon
Marseillaise	A rare version of this pattern shows a lady in a gown ushering two children.	Rare

Pattern	Description	Rarity
Mayfield	Underglaze printed in pale blue/white.	Uncommon
Nanking*	Underglaze printed in blue/white in a chinoiserie scene.	Uncommon
Pagoda	Underglaze printed in blue/white in a chinoiserie scene.	Rare
Potato	A common form of decoration (spongeware), usually accomplished by young children.	Rare
Puzzle Jugs	These are usually museum items.	Rare
Pekin	Underglaze printed in blue/white in a chinoiserie scene.	Rare
Treacle Jars	Underglaze printed in blue/white usually family heirlooms.	Rare
Pots showing the initials R.D. W.D. and S.D.	Family heirlooms belonging to the Dixon family of Whitehaven.	Rare
Willow	A standard willow pattern underglaze printed.	Common

---

* *An incorrect spelling*

REFERENCES AND BIBLIOGRAPHY

Sources
Original documents
Much of the early history of the West Cumberland potteries can be found by researching the archives of the Lowther family especially the papers of their Whitehaven estates D/Lons/W held at C.R.O. Carlisle, in particular the Eighteenth Century Rentals 1698, 1700-22 and the Estate Accounts book, Stewart's accounts and Cash book. (For details see Volume I by Florence Sibson published in 1991). These include several leases for land taken out by potters especially at Whitehaven and in the Dearham area. Quarter sessions papers were also useful.

Newspapers
Cumberland Pacquet 1774-1915.
Whitehaven News 1854-todate.
Whitehaven Gazette 1819-20 for shipping lists showing imports and exports.
Cumberland News article by Dennis Perriam on Carlisle pottery 21st Nov., 2003.

Directories of Cumberland especially
Parson and Whites 1829.
Mannix and Whellan 1849.
Bulmer 1884 and 1901.

Maps
Ordance Survey maps for Cumberland, especially the first edition *c*1860-1865.
Andrew Pelin's map of 17th century Whitehaven in the Lowther archives.

Parish Registers
The originals are kept at the Cumbria Record Office, Carlisle. CRO(C) for parishes north of the River Derwent and at the Cumbria Record Office and Local Studies Library, Whitehaven. C.R.O. (W) for those south of the river.

Articles and guides
Northern Ceramic Review.
Northern Ceramics Society Quarterly Newsletters.
E.C.C. Transactions Vol.9 Part 1, 1773 and Vol. 10 part 1, 1976 for
Elizabeth Adam's articles.
Official Guide to Osbourne House, Isle of Wight.

Catalogue of the contents of The Mint Museum, Charlotte, Carolina, U.S.A.

Antique Collectors Magazine
Collecting Ceramics of the 1840-1870 period
Article by Rosalind Pulver, Dec., 1998.

Ceramic Review
No. 12 December, 1971 *Gault Clay.*

Post Medieval pottery Vol V (1971)
Pottery making in London and Whitehaven in the 17th century by Lorna Wetherill and Rhoda Edwards.

Edwards, Dianna
Greenwood, Black basalt, Wedgwood and contemporary manufacture.

Books

Angerstein R.R.   *R.R. Angerstein a Swedish Industrial spy who travelled throughout Great Britain in 1753-56* published by The Science Museum in 2002.

Berthoud, Michael   *A Compendium of British cups.* Published by Micawber Publications, 1990.

Brears, Peter   *English country potters.* Published by David and Charles, 1974.

Finlay, Michael   *Western Writing Implements.* Published by Plains Ltd., 1990.

Godden, Geoffrey   *An Encyclopaedia of British Pottery and Porcelain Marks.* Published by Barrie and Jenkins, 1964.

Hainsworth, D.R.   *The correspondence of Sir John Lowther of Whitehaven 1693-1698.* British Academy Records of Social and Economic History New Series 7, 1983.

Lee, Revd Roger   A short guide to *Wesleyana and Methodist pottery.* Published by the Revd. Roger Lee in 1988.

May, Jonathan   *Commemorative ware 1780-1860.*
and Jennifer   Published by Scriber and Sons, 1972.

Miller, Prof.   *A Chronology of English Shell Edge, Pearl and*
George L.   *Whiteware 1989.*

Miller, Prof.   *English Shell Edged Earthenware, alias Leeds Ware,*
George L. and   *alias Feather Edge.*
Hunter, Robert R.

Miller, Prof. George L. and Smart Martin, Dr. Anne — *The Market Basket of Ceramics typically available in Country Stores from 1780-1900.* University of Delaware Centre for Archaeological Research, 1976.

Priestman, Geoffrey H. — *Minton Printed Pottery 1796-1832 Endcliffe Press, 2001.*

Price, Jacob — *From France and the Cheasapeak, University of Michigan, 1973.*

Pugh, Robert and Gareth Hughes — *Llanelli Pottery Wales,* Published by Llanella Borough Council, 1990.

Riley, Noel — *Gifts for Good Children,* Published by Richard Dennis 1991.

Sibson, Florence — *The History of the West Cumberland Potteries Volume I,* Published by the author, 1991.

Tyson, Blake — *Some aspects of Whitehaven's development before 1700* A.M.S. Transactions N.S.30 1986.

INDEX OF NAMES